Fitting In

OTHER BOOKS BY NATASHA JOSEFOWITZ

*Paths to Power: A Woman's Guide
from First Job to Top Executive*

Is This Where I Was Going?

*You're the Boss! Managing with
Effectiveness and Understanding*

OTHER BOOKS BY HERMAN GADON

Effective Behavior in Organizations

Alternative Work Schedules

FITTING IN

HOW TO GET
A GOOD START
IN YOUR NEW JOB

Natasha Josefowitz
Herman Gadon

ADDISON-WESLEY PUBLISHING COMPANY, INC.
Reading, Massachusetts • Menlo Park, California • New York
Don Mills, Ontario • Wokingham, England • Amsterdam • Bonn
Sydney • Singapore • Tokyo • Madrid • San Juan

Many of the designations used by manufacturers and sellers to distinguish their products are claimed as trademarks. Where those designations appear in this book and Addison-Wesley was aware of a trademark claim, the designations have been printed in initial capital letters (e.g., Gore-tex).

Unless otherwise noted, all the poems are from *Natasha's Words for Friends* by Natasha Josefowitz, Warner Books, 1986. We are grateful to Warner Books for the permission to reprint them.

The material that appears on page 37 is reprinted with the permission of *Fortune* magazine (May 28, 1984).

Library of Congress Cataloging-in-Publication Data

Josefowitz, Natasha.
Fitting in: how to get a good start in your new job / Natasha Josefowitz, Herman Gadon.
  p.   cm.
  Includes index.
  ISBN 0-201-11653-7 (pbk.)
  1. Work.   2. Interpersonal relations.   3. Success in business.
I. Gadon, Herman.   II. Title.   III. Title: New job.
HD4905.J67 1988
650.1'3—dc19   87-28592
                                                              CIP

Cover photograph by George B. Gibbons/FPG
Cover design by Copenhaver Cumpston
Text design by Joyce C. Weston
Set in 11-point Meridien by Compset, Inc., Beverly, MA

BCDEFGHIJ-DO-898
Second Printing, October 1988

*To my children: Nicole, Margaret, and John
with much love, and in memory of
my much-loved son, Bill.*

Herman Gadon

*To my stepchildren, Nicole, Margaret, and John,
and my late stepson, Bill:
thank you for having taught me much
about fitting in.*

Natasha Josefowitz

We are a society on the move. Each year, on the average, 20 million Americans, or one out of five people who are working, change jobs, and another six million enter the labor force. Therefore, on every work day approximately 100,000 people experience their first day on the job.

CONTENTS

PREFACE

Natasha Josefowitz

We all write about our own issues in one form or another. One of my lifelong issues has been fitting in. Born in Paris of Russian parents, I was known as "the little Russian girl" on the playground. In school in New York, I was called "the French girl." I married a Swiss man and lived in Switzerland, where I was seen as "the American lady." When I returned to the States, I was known as "the Swiss woman." When I moved to the West Coast, I was "an Easterner." In other words, I was always from somewhere else, trying to fit in — to be one of them, to be in on the jokes, part of the group, wanting to be "an old-timer" and not always "the newcomer." Although few people may have experienced as many major geographical changes as I have, most people in America have moved to another part of town, gone to a new school, or taken a new job. Moving into a new situation is often incredibly difficult, not least because people usually underestimate the stress the relocation can create. Though everyone goes through school changes, job changes, and changes in family status, only a few manage to stay put and live out their lives in the place where they were born and raised.

Until my mid-thirties I was a traditional housewife and mother doing volunteer work; then I went back to school and became Columbia University's oldest student. At that time a student could not register for classes if she was more than thirty-six years old. Also at that time, most women who wanted careers had to choose nursing, teaching, or social work. And so I picked social work and earned my master's degree at age forty. Making the change from housewife to student was dramatic, to say the least. After I helped the children with their homework, I stayed up late to do my own. My friends were not particularly understanding when I refused dinner invitations because I was studying for an exam. My unavailability meant that I was no longer part of the crowd. At school I was looked upon as somewhat of an oddity, being "so old." Most students were single and did not have to worry about babysitters and sick kids at home. Under these circumstances, trying to fit in was impossible.

As soon as I earned my degree, we moved to Switzerland for my husband's business. I was teaching at the Lausanne School of Social Work, and trying to fit into Swiss academic life. As a caseworker, I also became part of a therapeutic team at the local child-guidance clinic. No matter how hard I tried, I remained an outsider in both places. All these people had gone to school together and had common experiences that I could not share. I remember these years as painful emotionally, but rewarding intellectually. I was working on my Ph.D., my students were learning well, and my clients were improving, but the real yearning was to "belong."

After my daughter married and my son finished college, I decided to leave Switzerland and return to the States. After twenty-five years of marriage, I was suddenly single again. I accepted a teaching position at the University of New Hampshire, where once more I tried to become a part of the community. Neither the faculty members nor their wives made it easy. I did not understand then that acceptance had to be earned; it was not just given. As the only woman in the organizational-behavior group, I could not be "one of the boys." As the only "faculty woman," I was not "one of the girls" when I met with their wives. I stayed in New Hampshire for six years, and although in time getting along became easier, I never really became "one of them."

While there, I acquired a new family: Herman Gadon, several in-laws, and four stepchildren. Two of the children were still teenagers, two were young adults; all had their own way of doing things. I wanted to meet everyone's expectations and fit in *right away*. When I did not find immediate acceptance, I was disappointed and thought that I had somehow failed. I did not know that this adjustment takes years.

While on sabbatical leave, we spent a winter in San Diego, California, and fell in love with the place, the sunshine, and the people. We both got appointments to teach in the College of Business at San Diego State University. In contrast to our experience in New Hampshire, however, friendships were not confined to our colleagues. We met people from many fields; everyone had come from somewhere else. Everyone was new, without family, without roots, without a common past, wanting friendship and intimacy. We all wanted to re-create a family. And so we did. A small group of us started meeting monthly for pot-luck dinners at each other's homes. Finally, I was not the *only* new kid; we *all* were. And so we accepted one another, supported each other, were there when tragedy struck, and were there to celebrate together. Although each of us has become part of a larger community, we continue to meet once a month.

With next to no literature available on the topic of being the new person in a group, I decided I wanted to make the ordeal of fitting in easier for others than it had been for me by providing clues, insights, and guidance on how to deal with being "a new kid on the block."

As a nationally syndicated columnist, I receive letters from readers with questions about difficulties in being accepted at work. And so I decided to undertake research on the phenomenon described as initiation and acceptance in the work place. My research led to some startling discoveries.

This book is the result of a two-part research study I have conducted over the past five years. For three years, while teaching both undergraduate and graduate management courses at the San Diego State School of Business, my students assisted in the research. More than three hundred students interviewed in depth more than 1,000 people from different fields and at different job levels about their experiences either of being new themselves (which could include a new job, a transfer, or a promotion) or being manager of a new employee.

As I read the interviews, patterns became discernible. I was able to identify the specific stages required in going from outsider to insider. Contrary to expectations, people and organizations made it anything but easy for newcomers to become part of a work team. In fact, we found the opposite. Many barriers to achieving membership were thrown up: by coworkers, by supervisors, by organizational norms and policies.

As the study progressed, I changed the design to focus on a phenomenon that, it became evident, was a significant barrier to integration: hazing at work. In the second part of the study, students were asked to analyze and comment upon a case of hazing, written from both male and female perspectives. Students interpreted the hazing event and explained how they would have responded if it had happened to them. As a result, participating students showed increased awareness of the issues of membership. Another benefit was marked improvement in the skills needed for entering new social and work situations. In other words, managing one's own newness was most often a skill that could be learned.

Thus, this book distills not only my personal experiences, but research efforts by a large number of students. Many colleagues who serve as consultants to varied organizations throughout the United States were willing to test and report on some of our hypotheses and suggestions for "fitting in."

As a frequent lecturer, I have the opportunity to talk with people from all over the country. By asking them to describe their first days and weeks at work, I have learned that at times acceptance is not possible no matter how charming or knowledgeable you may be. I have also found that awareness of the problem is a first step toward resolving it, for most people don't want to make others suffer.

The road from outsider to insider may be rocky, but it has identifiable steps. Knowing the pitfalls will not make them disappear, but it will make the crossing easier.

PREFACE

Herman Gadon

My parents died when I was seven, and with my sister I went to live with a great-aunt and great-uncle and their six children. My two younger brothers were sent to live with other relatives in a different city. My aunt and uncle showed a lot of generosity, for the Great Depression was on and it was not easy to feed two extra mouths. Living with them, I learned my first lessons about "fitting in." Although I knew my relatives, they had their own ways of doing things that were different from those I had known, and I had to learn to adjust.

In my family I was the oldest of three boys, which conferred a special distinction on me. In the family to which I went, I was the youngest child and had to adjust to that different place in it. I was in a strange new environment and took on an unfamiliar new role, with unknown consequences for behaving badly.

Although few of our readers have had to cope with loss of their parents at such an early age, they probably have had experiences in youthful life that have shaped their attitudes toward entering new situations. For Natasha it was being different from the others around her. For me it was coping with newness, and only my sister was there to encourage me. Having little support from persons close to me whom I could trust, or with whom I could test the validity of my perceptions, I learned to be tentative at first and quiet, careful not to offend, sharpening my powers of observation so that when I was noticed, I would be doing the right thing. My unconscious fear of rejection was quite strong, for it seemed to me that my survival hinged on being accepted.

Thus I learned to adopt a low profile in new situations. This style of entry seemed to protect me and minimized the risk of rejection. Like any virtue used to excess, however, this stance can be a vice. Observing before acting is often wise, but sometimes it is wiser to act more spontaneously. As I have gained awareness about my way of seeking acceptance and membership, I have discovered that I have more choices. When it seems appropriate to be active from the start — to be among the first rather than the last to speak in a group — I will do so. I like the freedom this knowledge gives me. It takes thought and deliberate decision to go against my natural inclination to wait and watch, but I no longer have to be the victim of those early life experiences.

The changes I've undergone in my life as an adult do not particularly distinguish me from other Americans. I have been mobile, averaging a major change every three years. When I was nineteen, I left my birthplace, Worcester, Massachusetts, to join the U.S. Navy. After three and a half years in the Pacific Theater in World War II, I returned to Dartmouth College to finish my undergraduate education in economics. I received my Ph.D. in industrial economics from the Massachusetts Institute of Technology, married, settled in Providence, Rhode Island, bought my first house, and within a few years was raising a family of four children. These were good years. I became general manager of a small wire and cable company, and left that position to reunite with two brothers and a brother-in-law to build a new business based on high-vacuum technology. Then at age forty, I took advantage of the shortage of skilled university teachers in business schools to return to academic life. As one of the first faculty members hired by the Whittemore School of Business and Economics at the University of New Hampshire, I took great pleasure in helping it become a first-rate institution. On a leave sponsored by MIT and the Ford Foundation, I spent a year as visiting professor at the Indian Institute of Management in Calcutta, helping the school to develop curriculum and staff. I was later selected by the Harvard Business School to assist it and IMEDE, a renowned international graduate school of management in Lausanne, Switzerland (to which the Harvard Business School was an adviser) to build an MBA program. I went to Iran with the Arthur D. Little consulting firm to help it develop a business school training executives for Iran's industrial modernization campaign and to the Hague, Holland, to teach in the Institute for Social Research. In each of these situations I had to adjust to the demands of new cultures that exacted high prices of those who did not meet expectations.

Many geographic moves and changes in roles, jobs, careers, and life-styles, including marriage and divorce, are a part of my history, just as they may be part of our readers' background. We are increasingly a society in flux. Except perhaps for being orphaned at seven, my experiences are not unusual, although they may differ from others'. On the whole, my experience in fitting into new situations is confirmed by all that we have learned from the many people we have interviewed in preparing this book. We hope that our readers can use what we have learned to help themselves and others in new situations.

ACKNOWLEDGMENTS

We want to thank the following people who have taken time out of busy schedules to read the manuscript or provide us with information. Their suggestions and insights have broadened our understanding of fitting in and made this a better book: Scott Alexander, Director, Corporate Controls, General Electric Company; Adam Aronson, Chief Executive Office, Mark Twain Bank; Tom Bernard, Qualcom; Bob Boeller, Hewlett Packard; Barbara Benedict Bunker, Ph.D., Associate Professor of Psychology, State University of New York at Buffalo; Caroline Campbell, Human Resource Development, Fluor Engineers, Inc.; Calvin Colarusso, Ph.D., Psychoanalyst; Carolyn Desjardins, Ph.D., Director, National Institute of Leadership Development; John Donnelly, Manager, Manufacturing, General Electric Company; Kate T. Donnelly, Manager, Organization Staffing, General Electric Company; Robert Ellis, Director, Human Resources, J.M. Smucker Corporation; Kyle Fairchild, Aerospace Engineer, NASA, Johnson Space Center; Peggy Hanley, Training Specialist, Staff Education and Development, UCSD Medical Center; James Hollinden, Manager, Electronics, General Electric Company; Debora Scholl Humphreys, Management Consultant, Career Options Consulting Services; Vern Jennings, Manager, Human Resources, Harrah's; Don Jones, Training and Safety Coordinator, San Diego Water Utilities Department; James F. Kelley, Jr., Assistant Vice President/Training and Development Manager, Great American First Savings Bank; Mildred C. Linskey, Manager, General Education and Administration, General Electric Company; Meryl Reis Louis, Ph.D., Associate Professor, School of Management, Boston University; Ralph Mann, Merdan, Inc.; Grace Miller, Staff Education and Development Office, UCSD Medical Center; Richard H. Perry, Loral Instrumentation; Jane Russell, President, Russell-Rogat Transition Specialists; Mario Scipione, General Instrument; Gwen Slattery, National Cash Register; Trude Sopp,

Ph.D., Manager, Organizational Effectiveness, City of San Diego; Jan Stallman, Management Services Officer, Department of Agricultural Economics, University of California at Davis; and Donna M. Stringer, Ph.D., Deputy Director, Washington Department of Licensing.

Herman Gadon wants to recognize the members of the Executive Program for Scientists and Engineers class of 1987 at the University of California at San Diego for their thoughtful comments. Natasha Josefowitz would like to thank both the graduate and undergraduate students in her Organizational Behavior classes as well as her Women in Management students at San Diego State University, 1980–1984. Dr. Josefowitz also wishes to acknowledge her graduate assistants, Eunis Christensen and Carolyn Drurie for helping to process the research data and Barbara Maxey for conducting the surveys.

We are especially indebted to Martha Moutray, our editor, who was always available and responsive to our needs. Her careful attention to detail, her skill, support, and encouragement made her a joy to work with.

We also want to express our appreciation for our assistant, Kati Mikes-Papp. She not only kept inputting and inputting the countless manuscript changes in our computer (what a blessing this machine is!), but she read and reread the content, pointing out the repetitions and the inconsistencies. She not only put in long hours, but did so with good humor and enthusiasm.

Fitting In

THE CHANCE TO RECIPROCATE

If every one of us
who looks good
makes the rest of us
look better
And if the rising tide
lifts all ships

Why do we still compete
instead of helping each other?
Need we keep others down
in order to elevate ourselves?

If I help you today
I will be helped tomorrow
because the world
is made up not only of rivals
but of people who would like
the chance to reciprocate.

Introduction

FITTING IN!!!

Most of us want to belong — to be part of a group. We need to be accepted. We want to be liked, respected, paid attention to, even loved. We want to be heard as well as seen, and we want to fit in.

Sometimes fitting in is easy. The question of membership is seldom an issue when you are born in a community and live there all your life. At other times, membership must be earned. People change jobs or move, and must acquire new friends and associates — not once, but several times in a lifetime. Some people have a knack for becoming known quickly and developing relationships. For others, fitting in can be a painful experience, taking months or even years, living with the possibility that they may never be completely accepted. Those who give up trying to fit in may become isolated from the group and look for satisfaction elsewhere, or they may become mavericks, exaggerating their differences from the other members of the group. They may take solace in feeling they don't need anyone, that they are better than the group members.

Fitting in is a universal and lifelong problem. It starts early in our lives, with the task of becoming a member of the family. Some children fit in better than others even within their families. It goes on with school, where those who belong to the popular groups are viewed, often with envy, by those who do not. Fitting in becomes even more of an issue after schooling is completed, when people start working. We may find ourselves in work groups in which acceptance or nonacceptance may make the difference between being able to accomplish our task well or being prevented from doing so. Each job change, each transfer, each promotion requires that we find a way to fit in. Every time a project gets started involving new members, some of whom may or may not have worked together, the members must deal with issues of membership.

Human beings are social animals, and our greatest punishment is being separated from our family or group. Our worst deprivation is losing contact with others; the ultimate rejection is ostracism and excommunication. Even our language expresses our deep need to fit in. We attach a value to belonging, and we talk about team spirit, group effort, being "in" or "out." We describe the work of belonging with phrases such as "rites of passage," "learning the ropes," "paying your dues," "passing muster," and "earning your stripes."

This book is focused on the issues that surround fitting in at work. It is in the work setting that some of the more decisive events of fitting in occur. People who are not accepted by their coworkers are seldom happy in their jobs and have little opportunity to become productive employees. Although the major part of the book is directed to new employees, we also address issues faced by managers, group leaders, and policy makers in both small and large organizations. Even though in much of the book we deal with issues of newness from the perspective of the new employee, in the last chapters we offer guidance for managers of new employees. Subordinates and bosses must understand the other's point of view, for in all likelihood the new employee will some day become a boss, and the boss will become a newcomer in another job. The steps in integrating new people into the work place and in other settings must be thought through and dealt with in order to understand better the dynamics of helping people fit in more quickly. Only then can they become productive members of the group, sharing the feelings of loyalty and commitment that true membership generates.

Critical as it is to fit in, few guidelines have been found on how to do it. The task is usually very difficult, often quite painful, yet most people do not understand what is happening to them, or why. Do you remember the first day on your first job? Or perhaps you think back to the first day after that big promotion, or when you moved and became the new kid on the block. If you have been with the same organization a long time, you may work on different projects and move in and out of on-going work groups, or you lead projects with all-new members. Whatever your situation, you probably lived through a moment when you didn't know the rules, or didn't know the people, or were not sure how to behave; you didn't know what to expect from others, or even worse, what *they* expected of you. That moment of fear and confusion was probably during your first day, a time that made a lasting impression on you while you were making that all-important first impression on others. You had eight hours to form an initial opinion about your place of work and the same eight hours to give to others an idea about the kind of person you are.

A lot more happens on the first day than appears on the surface. People sniff each other out, start testing one another; some will engage actively in a conversation, others observe silently from a distance. How will each be to work with? Can that other be trusted? Will they collaborate or compete? Can you be up front or will you be taken advantage of? All these are unanswered questions: How do you find out? What do you look for? Whom do you ask? How do you become familiar with the unfamiliar? How do you get to be an old shoe and not feel your toes pinched every time you take a tentative step? How can you integrate better into the work place? How can you become effective faster — feeling "at home," part of the work group, a good team member?

The memories of some of our own first days at work, and in other new situations, are often quite negative. We felt isolated, not understanding the norms, not wanting to ask questions that we feared might have obvious answers. Anxiety, frustration, upset, and anger were common feelings as we experienced our own newness in varied situations.

While investigating different aspects of management for other research studies, we have continually encountered stories about people's difficulties integrating into the work force, about being alienated from the others, not being accepted by a group, feeling inadequate, or being the object of ridicule. As we began our inquiry about these first days at work, we heard more and more dismal accounts of poor or nonexistent orientation for new workers or new managers, lack of information about the job, about the employer's expectations, about the organization itself. We also found that first impressions lingered much longer than we would have expected, and that these impressions influenced the way people felt about their colleagues and their company for months, and sometimes even for years. These first impressions go both ways — how the new arrival perceives the work climate, and the lasting opinions that bosses, peers, and subordinates form about the new arrival. Our studies indicate that employers give remarkably low priority to the need for orienting new workers. Employers assign very little in time, budget, and personnel to the task.

In the last part of the book we give examples of orientation programs, all the way from small work places that add a new employee every few years to larger companies accustomed to orienting dozens of new employees every month. Supervisors, managers, and executives all need to make the work setting a welcoming place as well as to create policies that will make integrating new employees into the work force quicker and easier.

Our intention is to provide insights, information, and guidance to all those new kids on the block, their immediate supervisors, and their CEOs, so that life at work will be both pleasanter and more productive. Only by understanding what affects membership and what will make acceptance into a group easier, can anyone influence that process.

The key to fitting in is knowing what to do, when to do it, and with whom to do it. This book will give you that key.

THE IMPORTANT PEOPLE

I used to watch
the important people having lunch
wishing I could eat
with them

I used to wonder
what the important people said
wishing I could talk
to them

I wanted to know
where the important people went
wishing I could go
with them

I tried to guess
what the important people did
wishing I could do it
with them

And now that I have lunch with them
and talk with them and go with them
I've discovered that they look important
only from a distance

The important people
are no different from the people
who sat with me
when I used to watch
the important people
having lunch.

The Process of Fitting In: Exclusion and Undesirable Assignments

FIRST JOBS, TRANSFERS, OR PROMOTIONS

Whether you are starting your first job or your tenth, whether you're sixteen and bagging at the local supermarket or forty-five and taking on the presidency of a Fortune 500 company, you are about to become the new kid on the block. Whatever their rank or work setting, people entering a new or changed job situation share the same anxieties, the same feelings. They all hope to do well, to understand the needs they have been hired to meet, to get along with their superiors, their peers, or their subordinates. They hope to enjoy their work, have an opportunity to use their knowledge or skills, and be valued for their contribution.

In approaching that all-important first day, different people have different apprehensions. A young person may wonder what the others are like and whether he will get along with them. He may worry about making mistakes, and hope that his boss will be understanding. The senior manager may wonder if she will be able to get the information she needs in order to make the correct decisions. She may worry if the people who will be reporting to her can be trusted, and if political and economic conditions will enable her to show an early profit and earn credibility. She may be uneasy about her ability to beat the competition, be innovative, take care of the customers, and create a good work climate. An older woman returning to work after raising a family may worry about the gaps in her résumé and her need for retraining. If she is the oldest one in the department, she may worry that everyone will treat her like a mother or that she will not fit in at all.

A young, attractive woman may wonder if she will be subjected to sexual remarks, or be discounted as just a pretty thing. A minority person may fear possible discrimination. In spite of their different jobs, ages, sexes, and backgrounds, all these people want to do well.

They are anxious about fitting in, and they are hopeful that they will be happy at work. Their superiors are hoping they will be productive.

If you are a newcomer, you want to know how to help yourself. If you are the manager of a newcomer, you want to know how to help your new employees be happy *and* productive quickly. Yet, in spite of good intentions you, the newcomer, instead of feeling welcomed, feel like an outsider. No one seems to care; everyone is too busy to take the time to be helpful. Your boss does not explain anything, and it's not clear what you're supposed to do. Not only are people not helpful, but you feel as if you are in an enemy camp. Your coworkers talk in acronyms, and people seem to whisper about you, or even laugh outright at you. You are the butt of jokes; you are asked to perform menial tasks. What is going on?

You are going through the ritual of becoming a member. You are being excluded, and given undesirable jobs. You may even be hazed! For no matter how wonderful you as a newcomer may be, no matter how skilled at entering groups, how expert, charming, compatible, and helpful you may be, you will experience some kind of passage, a transition from outsider to insider, from newcomer to member, and eventually to oldtimer.

In our study of the fitting-in process, we identified three main stages that occur during the early days, weeks, and sometimes even months of a person's entering a new work setting. They may occur separately or simultaneously, and we call them exclusion, undesirable assignments, and hazing.

Excluding newcomers from the group and giving them menial or unrewarding work seems to be part of our culture. That's how newcomers are generally treated. It is not intended to create hardships. New people by definition undergo a learning curve and cannot be given a lot of responsibilities at the beginning. They must start slowly even though some may get impatient. Also, seniority has its privileges, including allocation of tasks. Those privileges are earned gradually. Hazing, however, is a different story. The unspoken intent is to *test* new persons to see how they will fit in. The newcomers are excluded on purpose to *teach* them the value of membership. They are *teased* and given humiliating tasks to see if they have a sense of humor and are willing to pay the price of membership.

Hazing is a test of loyalty, team spirit, and reliability; its purpose is to provide a rite of passage from newcomer to member.

STAGE I: EXCLUSION

Let's start with exclusion. It is the nonacceptance of the newcomer into the group, usually out of unintentional neglect. People are busy and forget to pay attention to the new person in their midst. The following case is a good example of one newcomer's poorly managed first days on the job and the unconscious exclusion, which resulted in a new doctor's experiencing a frustrating and difficult beginning.

We interviewed a young medical doctor on her first job on a hospital staff after finishing her studies. She spoke with bitterness about her first days at work. She was given no floor plan of the hospital; it would have helped her immensely to know where the labs and X-ray department were. A list of the hospital staff's names and positions would have helped her remember who did what. On top of feeling lost, she found her first week's schedule so full that she didn't even have time to go to the cafeteria for lunch and meet some of her new colleagues. They, in turn, did not offer to help her, so that she felt like an outsider for several weeks, and began to doubt her wisdom in having accepted this job.

A few changes in the process would have made a large difference. If her superior had not been too busy to pay attention, he would have noticed how isolated the young doctor was feeling. Floor plans inscribed with the names of the people working in each area would have been helpful to her, and should be given to all newcomers. A new employee's work schedule should never be so packed in the first week on the job as to leave no time for meeting and socializing with other staff members. In fact, meeting future colleagues should be facilitated by management, arranging a time when newcomer and coworkers can get to know each other. This plan is especially needed where teamwork is desirable.

Many organizations are understaffed and the employees overworked. When a newcomer arrives, people are relieved and a heavy amount of work is dumped on the unsuspecting new worker, risking overload. If the initial integration is poorly managed, or as for the doctor, totally neglected, the price is high in workers' dissatisfaction and low morale.

The appropriate response by the new employee to this exclusion phase is understanding that what is going on has nothing to do with anything the newcomer is doing. At this stage, newcomers have a tendency to feel hurt or angered, and to behave in a manner that only reduces their chances of inclusion: they pout, withdraw, or become disagreeable, responding in kind and not offering to help others in their tasks. Nor do they ask for help. This neglect is generally a mistake, because asking for help makes the person who gives it feel valued. Part of the confusion for the newcomer is the contradiction inherent in the exclusion phase. On the one hand, people are *verbally* welcoming; on the other hand, their *actions* belie their words.

We want to emphasize that even though the new employee's experience of exclusion may seem to be solely management's responsibility, and that the lack of preparation was not intended, the result is the same as if it had been purposefully planned. In other words, sins of omission are no more excusable than those of commission. We believe that responsibility is shared by all those who witness dysfunctional behaviors and who, by their unwillingness to speak up, become perpetrators as well.

Learning the Ropes

It is in the early days and weeks that one most needs to learn the ins and outs of the organization. We call the task "learning the ropes," which means learning not just the official rules and regulations, but also the unwritten rules, also known as norms. We must go beyond just learning the job; we must learn *how* the job gets done. In some settings, the job must be done quickly even if poorly; but in others, it must be performed meticulously even if slowly. A job well done is thus defined by the value systems of the people at work who create the philosophy of the organization.

The outsider is the person who does not *yet* know how things are done. The new employee must learn whether to address superiors by their first or last names, to eat lunch with people from other departments, to stay late and show commitment or to keep a messy desk, demonstrating great activity.

During this time, though, newcomers are not given this necessary information and are not allowed to participate so that they can observe and learn for themselves. One would think that to integrate new people into the organization quickly, everyone would bend over backward and make it easier by including the new people in activities, talking to them, and explaining procedures. In fact, the opposite often happens. The new employees coming from the outside are kept at arm's length and made to feel like outsiders. They are assigned menial tasks, such as staying to answer the phone during lunch hour, or asked to research something, spending long hours buried in papers. They are not asked to participate in group activities, and thus remain isolated from the others.

Most companies have stated policies intended to integrate a new employee quickly and easily into the permanent work group. Much that happens in the first days and weeks on the job, however, makes that integration difficult, if not impossible. We found this condition in comparable work settings in Europe, South America, and Asia.

The newcomer faces a difficult time indeed. Persons new to a job would like to feel welcomed and to belong instead of feeling isolated. The suffering that some newcomers go through in this stage cannot be underestimated. The following practices are tasks and experiences common to newcomers, according to the hundreds of people we interviewed:

1. Having to come earlier and stay later than the others.
2. Not getting a lunch break.
3. Being asked to answer phones while the rest go out to eat.
4. Being excluded from the organization's social activities.
5. Finding that the others talk in a code so that the newcomer is unable to participate in the conversation; that oldtimers tell in-jokes, referring to unknown people and events, or use unfamiliar acronyms.

The period varies during which one is kept out of the mainstream of events at work. For some people, this period may never end; they are never accepted or remain outsiders for years. They may be kept out by forces beyond their control, like being a woman in a tradi-

tionally male work environment, or being the only black or Hispanic working with whites. This may be because of personality
factors, perhaps the new employee is perceived as too different from
the others to be accepted. We know of an all-Italian work group in
a New Jersey plant that could never accept a non-Italian as a member of their group. This sort of exclusion is actually a form of harassment; continued noninclusion or purposeful rejection is indeed
as painful as active harassment.

For most people, the exclusion phase takes anywhere from one
day, or one week, up to a month, or even to six months.

One category of people, however, seems to remain on the outside
no matter how long they have been with the organization. They are
the ones whose work takes them away from home base so often
that whenever they return, they feel like strangers. They may be
sales representatives or consultants, or workers who are shifted
from project to project at different locations and with different people. These individuals can help themselves by

- Saying hello to everyone upon returning
- Eliciting information on what has been going on during their
  absence
- Giving information to relevant people about work-related
  matters
- Telling people they are close to about the more personal
  events they experienced while away
- Attending as many meetings as feasible to provide visibility
  for themselves
- Interacting with as many people as possible.

Employees who are frequently away have to reconcile themselves
to a special kind of membership. They may not always be aware of
or understand what is *really* going on. Even events that may seem
insignificant can affect the climate of the organization. The returning employee therefore needs to be cautious about making remarks
that may be interpreted as insensitive.

Dependence: What to Do

The initial weeks in a new job are the time of greatest dependence
upon others. This is the stage when the newcomer knows neither

the people nor the organization and needs to learn new skills. In the beginning, dependence is inevitable because not knowing the people, being unfamiliar with the physical layout, and not knowing the norms makes one dependent upon others for the information. This is often an uncomfortable time because most people prefer to be independent and autonomous. In our culture being dependent means being vulnerable, and we have been taught to avoid this exposure at all costs.

Newcomers at this stage depend upon others to teach them. This dependency can take varied forms, such as a specific skill or knowledge of the organizational culture. We cannot acquire understanding about how things are done by reading or listening alone; we can also learn by observing others, watching for clues, and being attentive to subtle cues. Being a good observer is critical during this period.

The two important factors during the stage of dependence are the attitude of the newcomer and the oldtimer's behavior toward this newcomer. Some new people take on the role of "bewildered learner," and behave as if they know nothing ("Please show me. Please teach me."), playing on their newness to make them appear as the "young, helpless things." One reason some people fall into that role is that as learners they are not held responsible for their mistakes. A mature and professional attitude would be to acknowledge the dependency and ask for help directly by saying: "This is something I don't know. I need to learn about it. What are the best ways for me to do so? Can you either help me or show me where I can get the information I need?"

First impressions do last, and the newcomer may be perceived as a dependent learner way beyond the learning stage. Confronting the issue by saying, "I feel excluded; tell me what to do to be accepted as a competent worker" may be a strategy to be used after enough time has elapsed. It takes a lot of self-confidence to do this. Accepting this period of trial with the knowledge that it will end should help to keep one's spirits up.

The dependence stage is an appropriate one for all newcomers to pass through. It is also a valuable time because during this period you can ask questions that you really can't ask as well later on when people won't understand why you haven't yet learned the task or the procedure.

Handling Exclusion

In most work settings, the message coworkers communicate to the new person in their midst is: "This is the way we do things around here." Usually, that message is unspoken and is more often communicated through body language. The cues are subtle, including such actions as raising eyebrows, shrugging shoulders, or audibly sighing when the nonconforming behavior occurs. The newcomer should be sensitive to these messages, which hint that the behavior is not well received. (Other messages, such as smiling, nodding, and eye contact are rewards for "doing the right thing.") Asking too many questions or disagreeing openly during a meeting may elicit a curt answer or a negative shake of the head, thus giving the sense that the questions or statements were either ill-timed or formulated incorrectly. The newcomer will have to learn to listen to how others communicate during meetings, which may be different from the way they talk to one another informally.

It is easier to correct one's behavior when negative feedback is available than when there is none. Sometimes the newcomer is given little or no help, feels isolated, and has no way of knowing what he or she is doing wrong. The issue may be the newcomer's personality, but it may also be a way of keeping out the new person, whoever it is. Either way the newcomer must conceive of ways to be acceptable and become accepted. Do people joke? Then join in the joking. Are people task oriented? Then be that, too. Are people formal? Then behave accordingly. In time, you become an insider, and can risk being different yet still be part of the group.

Although during this period of fitting in, it may feel like you are losing your integrity, even your identity, remember it is only a temporary situation. You must learn to play by the rules in order to enter the game. Once you're in, if you don't like the rules you can try to change them.

During this time, the oldtimers can make an enormous difference by being aware of the newcomer's need to learn and by actively offering help. We recommend the buddy system, assigning one person to be in charge of the newcomer's integration into the group. One person will answer questions, provide explanations, and guide the newcomer through the phase of "newness." One person, well regarded by the rest of the group, can help immeasurably during the early exclusion stage by bringing the newcomer along and shepherding him or her through the mazes of unknown and unfamiliar people and tasks. Acceptance, then, is bestowed sooner because a respected oldtimer is given the responsibility for integrating the newcomer into the work group.

STAGE II: UNDESIRABLE ASSIGNMENTS

A major problem for new employees is the likelihood that they will be assigned the jobs no one else wants to do. Newcomers are often stuck with the least interesting or rewarding jobs, the worst shifts, the most unpleasant clients or customers, the oldest cash registers, the poorly maintained trucks. They are asked to get coffee for others and are assigned the boring and menial tasks. This stage is known as *paying your dues.* The new person goes from outsider to lowest person on the totem pole, sometimes concurrently with the exclusion stage, sometimes right after it. In other words, you are not kept apart any more, but you are the person with lowest status and you are on probation. Sometimes just being there long enough will be seen as paying your dues. Time itself can count toward acceptance as a member, although the wait can make you feel like you are "doing time." In other words, you must spend an unspecified time at your place of work, doing the less interesting jobs, deferring to the senior members of the work group, and generally being willing to be the "low person on the totem pole."

This stage can run from a few days to a year or longer. The longest such experience we know of is that of a cub reporter who repeatedly pulled the poorest assignments for his first five years on the newspaper.

As the new person we learn our place in the organization's hierarchy by doing the work no one else wants to do. Will the person pay the dues willingly and respect the privileges held by the more senior members? Even U.S. Supreme Court justices are not immune. An article in the *New York Times Magazine* reported Supreme Court Associate Justice Blackmun's experience during his early years on the Court. "His lowly seniority, which garnered him assignments writing opinions in tax cases and other mundane fare, did not raise his profile."[1]

Paying Your Dues

As a newcomer is hired, the former low member on the totem pole moves up one rung and can now pass the scut work or grunt work, as it is sometimes known, to a more recent arrival. One privilege of seniority is not having to do the more undesirable duties. We interviewed two engineers who complained that, as newcomers, they were assigned trivial tasks or cleanup work on projects directed by senior personnel. They found this humiliating, a waste of their time and talent. One said: "Having been challenged in school to do my best and take on the most difficult tasks, and to be used now in such low-level work, is not only disconcerting but downright antagonizing." Another said: "They won't let you contribute until you've been around for a couple of years; by then my ideas will be outmoded." Their superior responded: "We have to know that a new worker can operate in a structured environment. All my workers, including myself, started out this way."

Doris, the only female fish cutter in a restaurant, was asked to do the heaviest labor, such as lifting pans and bags of fish. She was also told to clean all the cutting boards and drains. She felt she had to prove she had the strength necessary to lift the heavy loads and the willingness to do the menial tasks. Only after she proved she could do so was she accepted in the group. The same is true for rookie firefighters who must clean the bathrooms, sweep the dorms, polish the fire engines. At some stations, they are expected to respond to commands with "Yes, sir!" These examples of low-status task assignments resemble the experience of immigrants to this country. It is always the groups most recently arrived in a country who perform the more undesirable jobs at the lowest end of the pay scales. In the history of America, each immigrant wave has had its turn.

The best way to handle being assigned undesirable duties is to understand how common the practice is and that no one means it to be punishment for the individual. In other words, accept the tasks as part of the price of being a new employee and do them gracefully. When a task becomes burdensome and no new employee is coming along who can take it over, you might try the confrontation technique and explain to your coworkers: "Okay, guys, I've been doing this job long enough. Let's take turns now." For most people, passage of time alone solves the problem.

Exclusion, undesirable assignments, or menial work can cause new people to leave a job. We found that approximately 10 percent of the people we interviewed quit before they could be integrated into the work group. Many said that had they known at the time that their unpleasant experiences were just part of the organization's culture and not meant to single them out, they would not have left. For most, exclusion seemed to cause the most pain; menial work created the most humiliation.

Membership is an issue of everyday life. We like to feel "in," but then by implication some people must be "out." The more exclusive the group, the better the members feel about being part of it. Still today we have the phenomenon of exclusive men's clubs in which women are not accepted. The exclusion has nothing to do with competence or position, but only with gender. Similar arrangements occur at work: people who are already working together have formed special bonds and don't want the status quo changed by a stranger's intrusion. Those feelings are only strengthened if that stranger is of a different gender, race, social class, education, or age.

Learning the ropes and paying your dues may take a long time. Some of the ways we have found that people gained membership were: (1) finding something in common with a member of the senior group, such as sharing interests or having an acquaintance in common; (2) doing favors and accepting a probation period; (3) not moving in too quickly, assuming membership not as a right but as a privilege. If probation continues beyond a reasonable time or beyond what you can tolerate, then you should address the issue head-on.

Are you just going through a rite of passage, which will end in membership after you have been at the new job long enough? Or are you being harassed because coworkers don't want you? It isn't always obvious. If you are being harassed, then becoming part of the group will never be an option, no matter how long you are there.

Labeling

Newcomers get labeled very quickly. One study shows that within thirty seconds of meeting someone, people are already forming general impressions.[2] It does not take much time to become known as a person who does this or that, has this characteristic or that habit. If you refuse to help someone because of pressure from your own deadline, you may be labeled "uncooperative." If you have not disclosed privileged information in spite of pressure to do so, you may be labeled "trustworthy." Some supervisors expect their subordinates to demonstrate commitment by coming in early and staying late. Others may feel that working overtime means the job is not under control, that you are disorganized.

Another type of labeling goes on in the work place: the tags people attach to those they do not know. We are all familiar with the sometimes negative stereotypes people have of young people, old people, members of religious groups not their own, and racial or ethnic minorities, but there are others. According to an article in *Time*, MBAs "are often seen as inexperienced, arrogant, highly individualistic operators, with no patience for team effort."[3] Newcomers need to realize that some places of work may be prejudiced against employees with advanced degrees; other places may be equally prejudiced against workers who lack them. The labeling may be a function not of anything the newcomer does, but rather what the newcomer is. Stereotypes can be dispelled only with time. This tendency for stereotypes to persist is one of the reasons a newcomer's behavior in those first days is so critical.

FITTING IN FROM DAY ONE

Here are a few guidelines to help you deal with those first days on the job and avoid being labeled because of some early behaviors, which, by the way, may not be at all typical of you, but which will stick in spite of evidence to the contrary.

1. Do as your boss does — observe what seems to be important to him or her so that you are seen as understanding priorities.
2. Do what your boss wants — even if you disagree; be creative only if you are sure originality will be seen as an asset.

3. Overprepare for all initial meetings so that you will be seen as someone who does your homework.
4. Meet all deadlines so that you will be known as dependable. Beat your own deadlines if you can.
5. Do not promise anything you are not l00 percent sure you can deliver.
6. Keep your desk neat and your filing system current, unless a cluttered desk is a sign that people are productive.
7. All your paperwork should be free of spelling and typographical errors, with no erasures even in draft form. This neatness matters at the beginning because material that is written is judged first by its appearance, and second by its content.
8. Be outgoing and project an image of yourself as a good team player.
9. Show competence, but don't talk about how "we" did it at Company X unless asked.

Remember that however you are labeled in the beginning, the tag will stick and influence the course and success of your career.

We have observed that frequently a new manager will want to make changes in staff or operations immediately. Just as animals mark their territory, new managers want to make their mark and distinguish their new turf from their predecessor's. New managers may start off by rearranging their office; moving desk, bookshelves, chairs; putting pictures on the walls and family photos on the tables. Some changes are all right, but go slow. Starting to make changes too early in the office, plant, or laboratory, rearranging others' schedules, shifting responsibilities among one's staff should be delayed until manager and staff have mutual knowledge and the beginning of trust and credibility between them.

PASSING MUSTER AND EARNING YOUR STRIPES

As newcomers learn the ropes and pay their dues, they pass from dependency to autonomy. Tasks can be accomplished now without help. The responsibilities can be met. The environment makes sense, and the newcomers are beginning to feel a little like insiders. They are not yet full-fledged members, however; insider status is not given lightly. The newcomers must now pass muster. In this next and final stage they are tested to see if their performance is up to standards and if the personality fit is good.

If the newcomer's performance is exceptional, problems may arise with peers, perhaps because of excellent productivity. If performance is average and personality problems become evident, chances are the newcomer will be discharged unless a labor shortage means his or her specialty is scarce. If the newcomer's personality fits in well with the rest of the group, average performance probably will be acceptable. On the other hand, performance below par can eventually lead to dismissal. In many organizations, though, exceptional performance is so highly valued that an eccentric personality can be overlooked.

Membership and seniority are privileges that must be earned, and the newcomer must pass through stages to achieve them. The third and most difficult stage we call "hazing" or "passing muster," and it can be concurrent with or right after the first two phases.

HAZING

My first day on the job
I'm excited and hope they will like me
Why are they whispering in the corner?

Is it about me?
Did I do something wrong?
They make me nervous.

They're looking at me, laughing
Are my clothes not right?
I feel anxious.

They went off to lunch
And left me alone
I cried in the bathroom.

My boss came and asked if all was well
I said "Just fine!"
With pounding heart.

My machine jammed
Was it done on purpose?
I'm sick to my stomach.

At the end of the day
No one said goodby
I don't want to go back.

The Three T's: Teasing, Testing, Teaching

STAGE III: HAZING

The practice of hazing has always been associated with undergraduate fraternities and military academies. Yet many people experience a form of hazing in most kinds of work — from corporate offices, factories, and laboratories to all sectors of the economy, in government, industry, and service organizations. We were unaware of hazing in the world of work until we learned of the following event. Consulting to city administrators, one of the authors heard about the first female ever hired as a sanitation worker. After her first day at work, she complained of harassment. As she told the story, she had lifted a heavy trash can to dump the contents into the back of the truck. As she was about to tip it in, the driver observed her in his rearview mirror and drove off, leaving her off balance so that she spilled the contents onto the street. She became upset and complained to her supervisor that she had been harassed. In questioning the other employees, we found that she had experienced a common practice, done to all new employees on their first day. The men did not seem to think the incident unusual, but the woman to whom it happened thought she saw some form of discrimination.

Hazing of this sort has been mostly a male experience. Most men know that such pranks are inflicted on new people, expect them, and take them in stride. They have experienced hazing in fraternities, in the military, in team sports. Women, however, have little experience with hazing, and therefore take the acts personally, believing them to be aimed only at themselves. In other words, the men know they are being hazed and accept it as a part of the ritual for all newcomers; women, on the other hand, believe the same action is meant to harass them, and so they react more negatively.

Upon this discovery, we started interviewing people and for the next two and a half years collected data on hazing. We found that hazing at work is indeed a common practice, that it takes many forms, that it is directed at most newcomers, that it goes through specific stages, and that the newcomer's way of responding to the hazing influences the way in which the hazing progresses. We also found that most women are unaware of this practice and react more negatively than men do. Because it is so common an occurrence, targeted at both men and women, we feel that anyone entering a new group, their managers, and organizations in general, must understand these practices, the reasons behind them, the responses that work, and their functionality. Hazing's influence on productivity is immeasurable. The longer a new worker takes to become effective, the costlier the experience is to the organization. We in the United States, with a growing, heterogeneous work force, with women and minorities entering in large numbers, face an ever more acute problem with integration.

Interviewing people who had been severely hazed, we asked if they would go easy on others. By far the majority answered, "Why should they have it any easier than I did?" In other words, membership would be devalued by less demanding entry, and the struggle current members experienced in seeking acceptance would then lose its meaning. One purpose in all these experiences was to make newcomers value membership in the group by temporarily keeping them on the outside. The longer one is kept out of a group, the more appealing membership becomes.

We were surprised to find the sense of mastery that prevailed as people remembered their hazing experiences. Those who had "made it" felt that their stripes were well earned, felt proud of getting through the ordeals, and wanted to retain the exclusivity earned in that arrival by not making it easy on newcomers.

To understand the need for hazing newcomers as a requirement for membership in a stable group, we collected more than 400 hazing events and found them fitting into identifiable categories and specific phases. The purpose behind hazing was to socialize the newcomer in the ways of the oldtimers. Hazing is one means by which newcomers can become group members by going through a series of tests. The unpleasantness and duration of these tests depend on three factors:

1. How cohesive is the group? The tighter the group, the more difficult it is for new members to be accepted; the looser the group,

the less resistance they find in entering it. When they face not a group but an agglomeration of individuals who happen to work in the same place at the same time, then membership is not an issue, and hazing does not occur.

2. How different is the individual from the other members of the group? The greater the perceived difference (gender, race, background, education, religion, and so on), the more the person's competence and personality fit are tested.

3. How well does the individual respond to attempts to integrate him or her into the group's culture? (Accepting prevalent values, learning appropriate behaviors, acquiring necessary skills, and so on.)

Why Hazing Is Commonplace

Hazing is a way of gaining membership in a permanent group, accomplishing a number of goals for the group, by (1) Giving the senior members a way of establishing their seniority and dominance. (2) Ensuring that formal work regulations will be complied with, and that the organization's unwritten rules or norms will also be followed. (3) Pushing the newcomer into letting go any former identity and loyalty to another group or organization and into taking on a new identity as a member of the new group. (4) Ensuring continuity of existing practices. (5) Making membership in that system something to be valued. The more difficult the passage from outsider to insider, the more valuable that membership will be. Sometimes hazing can be so mild that it is hardly perceptible. At other times hazing can be dangerous, such as telling a construction worker that something is safe when it isn't.

Effects of Hazing

We must understand how hazing affects workers and organizations because, although it is common, its practices are seldom talked about. We know that hazing is part of the newcomer's experience, making it *critical* for all new employees to know that the practice exists, the forms it takes, and the responses that will provide them with membership.

Most members of a group prefer the status quo, things as they are now. A new employee coming into a group makes the members shift their relationships with one another. They face a new, unpredictable voice, an unknown person who has no loyalty to the group. The newcomer implicitly threatens to diminish the power and influence held by some members. Anyone new is thus a threat to the group's stability. Groups tend to react in order to prevent newcomers from rocking the boat, or from participating, until they understand better how the newcomers will affect the group. These rites of passage from stranger to member, from outsider to insider include tasks that are to be performed and appropriate behaviors that are to be exhibited in order to protect the group from too much disruption.

Some memberships that we are born into, such as being part of an ethnic minority, may result in either pride or shame, depending on how the group perceives itself within a larger, dominant culture. A group of senior citizens' only prerequisite may be age. Most groups, though, have rules, formal or informal, public or unconscious, on how to get in. Group membership is valued more if becoming a member is a privilege that must be earned. One can gain group membership by fulfilling specific obligations, such as doing volunteer work; or meeting set criteria, such as being president of one's company; or again by showing interest in organizations such as a golf club, bridge club, or medical association. The most difficult groups to enter are those established in an organization, without specific criteria or *known* rules for membership — otherwise known as organizational norms or unwritten rules. A newcomer's arrival pulls the older group members closer together because they feel more "in" when they face an "outsider."

We have studied groups as diverse as military academies, professional associations, sororities, faculty committees, construction crews, athletic teams, corporations, and service organizations, and found that most have some form of initiation rites. Some were obvious, others subtle. Wherever we found groups, we also found that entry into those groups consisted of an identifiable move from one stage to another. The quality that seemed to make a difference was how tightly knit the group was. In studying two banks in the same town, we found that one had almost no organizational culture, no team spirit, and no rite of passage for newcomers, but a great deal of turnover. It had no group to enter or be excluded from. In the other bank, employees had formed strong bonds to one another and newcomers were not welcomed.

Some people, however, are never excluded — others are excluded, but are not teased. Some people suffer terribly from hazing, but others are welcomed immediately. As we have seen, the way in which newcomers behave, being the new kids on the block, influences the type and length of hazing they will be made to endure. Knowing ahead of time what to expect will help newcomers make the right responses.

Definitions

The dictionary defines hazing as "to persecute or harass with meaningless, difficult, or humiliating tasks. To initiate by exacting humiliating performances from or playing rough practical jokes upon."[1] This sense is different from the one including "undesirable assignments," because scut work is often a necessary part of training or just a job that needs to be done. When an intentionally meaningless or humiliating task is chosen, it becomes a test and therefore a form of hazing. Is the person willing to endure the test in order to become a member? An employee who passes the test will eventually gain membership in the group, which is the purpose behind "hazing at work." We find it interesting that anthropologists refer to these events as "degradation ceremonies." In other words, it is a degrading task and a humiliating time.

Another side of this definition is the *conscious* decision to keep newcomers out of conversations, gatherings, and other events. We found a large number of people who were not directly persecuted, but who were kept out by their coworkers on purpose. These people suffered at least as much from this rejection as did those who were more obviously hazed. In other words, if a new arrival is intentionally and consciously excluded, then that act is hazing. If no one intends to reject the new person, but he or she is just not made to feel welcome, that is part of the exclusion phase. Even though the newcomer may suffer as much from unintentional exclusion as from intentional isolation, the difference is significant because it is easier to remedy neglect than to counter intentional rejection. If people are unaware of their actions, they may be only too glad to make an effort toward helping a newcomer adjust. If the snubbing is done on purpose, however, then it serves the group's need to remain exclusive.

There are many examples of hazing by exclusion. The newcomer's status as outsider is reinforced either by physical separation from the group or by symbolic separation. A newcomer may experience these actions during the exclusion phase:

- Derogatory comments are made about the new employee's clothes, speech, manner, or work habits.
- The victim is the butt of jokes.
- Crude wisecracks are made in front of women with explanations that it's "man's talk." Even the usual apology after using an obscene word or making an off-color joke casts the person apologized to as an outsider.
- Apprentices, teacher's aides, students are ignored by the more senior members.
- The newcomer is excluded for the first year from all social events and is denied privileges.
- The newcomer is consistently overlooked and disregarded and is told that his or her contributions are irrelevant.

If any of these behaviors continues for an extended period of time, they become harassment and should not be tolerated.

THE PURPOSES OF HAZING: TEASING, TESTING, TEACHING

The purpose of hazing can be summed up as the three T's — Teaching, Teasing, and Testing: *teaching* novices their place in the hierarchy (the pecking order); *teasing* the newcomers (can they take it?) to see whether their personality will fit in (will they belong?); and finally, *testing* the rookies for their competence, their loyalty to the group, their reliability as team members.

The differences among teaching, teasing, and testing lie in the perpetrators' intent. "Teaching" really implies issues of "seniority." Senior employees get pleasure from pulling rank, which reinforces their higher status. People enjoy being able to wield the power of deciding who will be excluded and who will be included; to have people "below" themselves makes them "high" in the pecking order. To have a low person on the totem pole reinforces others' feelings of being top dog. Our language is quite explicit in defining human hierarchies. We differ little from other animals that align themselves in a definite pecking order, for it is always the same chicken that gets to peck first, the same cow that leads the others to pasture, the same lion that has the largest pride, at least until a younger, stronger lion challenges the patriarch to a fight and wins that next step on the career ladder. When the newcomers are made to do humiliating tasks on purpose, to teach them who's boss around here, it is hazing.

The difference we found between "teasing" and "testing" is that testing really evaluates whether the newcomer can be relied upon, whereas teasing, also a form of testing, has only one purpose: to see if the newcomer has a sense of humor. Even though hazing is consciously done, many people seem surprised if confronted with their behavior as hazing. At first they are inclined to deny that they are hazing, but then they reluctantly agree that indeed they have been perpetrating an act to which they had not given a name.

Teasing

Teasing can be the goodnatured part of hazing. It may be quite harmless, creating a distraction and helping bond the newcomer to the group by providing a shared experience that is fun. We interviewed the president of a large aeronautics company who told this story: When he was still general manager of a division, his superior called him to a meeting at 5:00 P.M. on a Friday and told him to bring with him his calculations for the next quarterly budget. He did so with some trepidation and arrived to see the assembled staff with glum faces. He sweated on as questions were thrown at him until a large sign was placed on the wall announcing his promotion as president of the company. Everyone else had been in on the surprise, but the new president almost fell through the floor; the event is remembered with great glee by all who were present.

Teasing usually creates a situation inducing laughter. Laughing together reduces social barriers and is a means for socializing, bridging differences, and affirming common values. Humor can, however, be mixed with aggression. During hazing, hostilities bottled up by frustrated individuals can be released covertly yet legitimately.

No wonder those who've been hazed can't wait to have someone to haze in turn, thus both aligning themselves with the senior members and releasing their own aggression on the newcomer. It has been observed that, "Humor can provide at least momentary freedom from the constraints of our adult roles. Through jokes we can mention forbidden subjects, engage in offensive or childish behavior, and even step outside the bounds of good taste. In the playful context of a joke, every moral taboo can be violated — and if anyone challenges our behavior, we can always say "I was only joking!"[2] Strong laughter can create bonds between people, and that's where it can be especially useful at work. The urge to share a joke is almost irresistible. So important is the ability to laugh together that not being able to share a joke can stop a relationship from developing. We must be aware, however, that in any hierarchy the senior-level people joke most often; their targets often are the junior members. Junior people, on the other hand, rarely laugh publicly at the senior people, but instead set themselves up as targets for humor, thus ingratiating themselves with those in positions of authority. Newcomers in these situations have the role of juniors and must be careful who or what they laugh at.[3]

Laughing Examples

Let us see some examples of hazing in which the primary purpose is to tease the newcomer and incite laughter. A trick frequently pulled is sending the new employee to look for a nonexistent object: the lawyer researches a case which does not exist; the restaurant employee is sent to fetch the "bacon stretcher"; the police officer races to an address that is an empty lot; the draftsman tries to design an impossible object; the hospital orderly looks for a fallopian tube to bring to a room that isn't there. New employees have been asked to fetch such unlikely objects as striped paint, muffler bearings, pipe stretchers, left-handed hammers, and other non-existing tools. When the newcomers look for the object, they are told that some other person has it, and they are sent off to look somewhere else, until they finally catch on. Some pranks played on newcomers:

- gluing a telephone to a desk
- nailing a lunchbox to the rafters

ON THE FASTRACK

- giving an assignment to collect rent from a prostitute known to proposition rent collectors
- being told to join flight crew members in the middle of the night for an incorrect departure time
- giving a can of paint to shake whose top had been loosened
- emptying a vice president's office while he was away
- recording pornographic messages on a tape and watching while they are received
- putting a match to the news release being read by the new radio broadcaster
- locking a new stockboy inside the walk-in freezer for five minutes
- stealing a marching band's underwear and draping it over their seats
- putting eggs in a firefighter's boots
- greasing the handles of a new mechanic's machine
- filling food orders incorrectly
- being told to inventory pickle slices
- giving a new saleswoman going to a convention the name of a hotel in the red-light district
- hiding a sanitary napkin in the pile of hot towels to be distributed to airline passengers by a male flight attendant
- shooting a rubber band at a newcomer who is giving a presentation at a large ad-agency meeting
- telling a waitress that she is required to give a portion of her tips to the bartenders, when this was not expected of other employees
- telling subordinates that the new manager is the new typist

- sending a new inspector in the wrong direction to deliver messages to truck drivers; he is then blamed for getting lost
- inviting a new employee to join the group for lunch and leaving the newcomer with the bill
- ordering a new female police officer to frisk a female suspect who turns out to be a transvestite.

Testing

On the serious side, we find that the more dangerous the type of work, the more dangerous the testing of newcomers. A group needs to find out as quickly as possible if the new person can be relied upon as an effective team member when significant risks to the lives of the workers or the safety of a population are likely to come up. We found many ways in which the newcomer was unwittingly put to the test:

- When trial jumping from a test tower, paratroopers were fitted with one strap shorter than the other, making them fall lopsided.
- A new skilled machinist, the only one with a college education, was given a flawed piece of metal to fit into a drill press. Had he not paid attention, it might have shattered and injured him.
- Older employees tampered with the new employee's cash register, causing her to keep ringing up the wrong amount. At first she thought it was her fault, then realized that the machine was broken, and asked for help.
- The senior engineer handed a new engineer an instruction manual and told him to instruct himself; no further help was available, and he had to learn alone.
- A driver was given a vehicle low on gas and without an emergency brake. From then on, he checked vehicles for potential danger before driving off.
- An electrical contractor pushed a fish tape (a flat, flexible wire) through a pipe to a transformer, because he was told the transformer was not active; it was. He learned not to trust anyone else's word about whether the power was on or off.
- A biologist kept finding foreign specimens placed among his lab samples.

- A new faculty member was given contradictory information on what he needed to do to gain tenure.
- An equipment technician for a water utilities company deliberately left out one instruction when showing a trainee how to operate a jackhammer. The trainee pretended the tool worked fine until he mustered enough courage to get help.
- A new branch manager left the cash-drawer key out. A co-worker hid it, returning it only when the manager had become quite frantic. The key was never left out again.
- A new supervisor was not told about known problems, but was given a false sense of security and confidence.
- A trainee was asked to arrive at 4:30 A.M. on his second day at work to help rearrange the stockroom. The manager didn't show up until 9:30 A.M.
- A bank teller found extra cash in her drawer, planted there to test her honesty.

One of the more dramatic illustrations we have come across in testing newcomers engaged in dangerous work comes from *The Wall Street Journal*:

NATURAL ENEMIES: LOGGING IN THE NORTHWEST FORESTS IS A DAILY CONFRONTATION OF MACHO MEN WITH DANGER

Everyone who enters the woods is hazed crudely and unmercifully. Does he have big ears? He is Dumbo forever. Is he a newlywed? Slip some dirty pictures into his empty lunch box so his bride will find them. Put rocks in his gear bag, give him grueling, unnecessary chores to do. Test him.

In work so dangerous, it is vital to cull the unfit and the incompatible. A streak of meanness in the hazing often is the first sign that a man is on the way out. The victim may have his lunch destroyed or his clothes set afire; then another man may invite him behind a tree for a faceful of knuckles. Finally, the hook tender — the boss union logger — may simply say, "Go down the road. We don't want to see you anymore."

If a man is a good worker but cannot get along with his fellows, Mr. Coady will bluntly tell him he is fouling up and that if he can't adjust to his next crew, he will be run off. Bluntness is always the loggers' way. "It's good, clean communications, one-on-one," he says. "No dancing around, no politics. Logging is an open society, and that's one reason I like the industry so much." The woods are full of men who have repeatedly quit the miseries and dangers but who keep coming back. The open, rough camaraderie, the knowledge that they can do work others quail from out of fear or weakness, forges a sense of community they cannot find outside.[4]

Teaching

To teasing and testing, oldtimers often add hazing designed to teach a newcomer his or her place in the informal organizational hierarchy. This example from the playing field, probably familiar to many readers, reflects how much seniority means to people and the respect they feel it deserves. Here we quote Pat Curran, business manager of the San Diego Chargers, a professional football team:

> CHARGERS' HAZING DAYS OF SUMMER ARE NEARLY GONE
> At one time hazing rookies at training camp was common. As long as it's done in fun, it's a necessary miserable time that breaks the monotony of camp. Necessary for the veterans who thrive on taking advantage of their stature, and miserable for the rookies who are burdened with one more thing to be nervous about. Rookies still fear hazing tactics as much as ever, but most of the Chargers' veterans say that the real days of hazing are over. With the increase of salaries of young players, it's harder to demand a song from a player with a two-year no-cut contract and a $100,000 signing bonus. I still think it's good that you don't treat a rookie like a king; kick him in the butt a little bit. I used to kill Hank [Bauer], when he was a rookie; torturing Hank was the most fun because it was so easy. But I only would do things to the guys I liked. In a crazy sort of way, they also make a young player feel as if he is one of the guys and part of the team.[5]

Another example is from the high-pressure world of financial trading. In that environment hazing is used to speed a person's progress up the learning curve, because the dollar cost of ignorance is potentially so high:

> The women who have made it as traders all have *war stories* to relate. Many initially encountered hostility or ridicule from their male counterparts; others complain of being regularly jostled and pummeled in

the hurly-burly of the ring. Still, there is powerful incentive to persevere. Successful traders can earn $250,000 a year and a few make more than $1 million.

Some hazing, moreover, is a ritual for newcomers of both sexes. Beginners' errors cost other traders time, energy, and sometimes money, so novices are forced to learn quickly. "It's like any business," says Susan Cole, the twenty-six-year-old President of NCZ Commodities, Inc. in New York, "They want you to pay your dues."

But for women, proving one's mettle is especially difficult in an atmosphere akin to an NFL locker room. The jostling, the shouting and volatile outbursts of temper in the ring all reflect the extreme pressure on floor traders.[6]

Socializing the Newcomer

Socialization is the name for the entire successful progression of a newcomer, from entry and the experience of exclusion to the final earning of membership. As we have seen, hazing as a stage in socialization can be subtle and hardly noticeable, or severe and unpleasant. As part of socialization, hazing imposes humiliating or stressful experiences on an individual as a requirement for membership in a group, acting as a barrier one must cross. A recent article in *Fortune* describes hazing in business used not only to teach newcomers their place in the pecking order but also to reinforce team spirit by providing shared stressful events.

> Companies subject the newly hired individual to experiences calculated to induce humility and to make him question his prior behavior, beliefs, and values. By lessening the recruit's comfort with himself, companies hope to promote openness toward their own norms and values.
>
> This may sound like brainwashing or boot camp, but it usually just takes the form of pouring on more work than the newcomer can possibly do. IBM and Morgan Guaranty socialize with training programs in which, to quote one participant, "You work every night until 2:00 A.M. on your own material, and then help others." Procter & Gamble achieves the same result with what might be called upending experiences — requiring a recent college graduate to color

in a map of sales territories, for example. The message is clear: While you may be accomplished in many respects, you are in kindergarten as far as what you know about this organization.

Humility isn't the only feeling brought on by long hours of intense work that carry the individual close to his or her limit. When everybody's vulnerability runs high, one also tends to become close to one's colleagues. Companies sometimes intensify this cohesiveness by not letting trainees out of the pressure cooker for very long — everyone has so much to do that he doesn't have time to see people outside the company or reestablish a more normal social distance from his coworkers.[7]

ORIGINS OF HAZING

In trying to discover where and when hazing originated as a ritual for integrating newcomers, we surveyed the anthropological literature and found that the rites of passage from outsider to member were surprisingly similar whether in the bush or on Madison Avenue. In both instances, a stranger who wants acceptance passes through stages from outsider to insider with specific tests and ceremonies.

As we studied ritualistic behaviors connected with membership in groups, such as entering, gaining status, or leaving, we found that primitive tribes in Africa, medieval guilds in Europe, and corporate offices in the United States all have similar ways of assimilating new members. We also observed that contemporary behaviors and rituals, such as our habit of bringing flowers or wine when we are invited to dinner, may have roots in earlier cultures. In primitive tribes, strangers must prove their good intentions when they come into a village by bearing gifts and offers of food. The practice in some companies of giving bonuses to workers who have performed well may be a vestige of the royal duty that called for distributing gifts to loyal subjects. Bonuses or royal gifts are effective ways of creating continuous social bonds. The custom of giving employees a farewell reception, and a letter of recommendation, or an inscribed gold watch is similar to the custom of feasting a young man leaving the village and presenting him with a tribal symbol that will help incorporate him into other groups.[8]

Even the symbols of status, whether for king, tribal chief, head honcho, or chief executive officer (CEO), are not that dissimilar:

The palace	The lavish corporate headquarters
The throne room	The corner office
The throne	The large custom-designed desk and leather swivel chair
The royal robes	Made-to-order suits
The scepter	The inscribed gold pen or gavel
The tribal carving	The corporate logo
The royal barge	The corporate jet
Religious offerings	Contributions to philanthropic organizations
Personal servants	Administrative secretaries
Providing feasts and celebrations	Giving office parties
Rewarding with titles and territories	Rewarding with promotions and bonuses

As we see, patterns of human behavior are similar even though the societies are geographically, linguistically, culturally, and ethnically diverse. Some anthropologists believe that these behaviors may be genetically acquired traits that helped the species survive. In other words, initiation rites must be considered not as isolated events, but as a function of the human need to place people in categories. Newcomers arouse anxiety until they become known and can be labeled. Rites of passage are a necessary practice that eases the transition from one stage to another, from newcomer to group member.[9]

We can now begin to understand hazing as a device protecting tightly knit groups against intrusion by strangers until the group can be assured that the newcomer can be trusted and will fit in. Many animals that live in groups will not incorporate an individual of their species that is not part of their original pride, troop, or clan. We have seen accounts of stray animals that must live for a long time on the periphery of a group. In primitive societies, wariness of strangers must also have contributed to survival, perhaps by keeping the group's integrity or protecting the women and children.

THE PATH TO MEMBERSHIP

Anthropologists identify the stages in socialization as *separation, transition,* and *incorporation.* During *separation* a group of boys is isolated for a period from the rest of the tribe. We have called this stage "exclusion." The newcomers are outsiders, not allowed to participate in coworkers' activities. As anthropologists describe this separation stage, the initiate is isolated in a special hut, often outside the village boundaries, for a specified time and may be forced to wear body paint or feathers to differentiate him from the others.

In our culture, exclusion occurs for new workers, when they may be asked to wear a special badge (many of us remember the freshman beanie), attend orientation programs, and are kept at a distance until they know the ropes. Eventually, the newcomers can begin to take part, but even then they get the least interesting work. We have called this practice "undesirable assignments." Newcomers are now paying their dues. *Transition* is the testing period when boys must prove their manhood by showing courage, skill, and willingness to endure hardship. They are in transition: no longer boys, not yet men. Newcomers are no longer outsiders, nor yet members. We call this stage hazing. It is the time when the senior members, to make sure that their seniority is respected by discounting the newcomers, play jokes on them, and make them do menial tasks. They must pass muster. They are tested and teased.

There are surprising similarities between hazing practices in primitive tribes and in the United States today:

- Out in the bush, as part of his initiation into manhood, the boy is given a riddle that has no answer. When he cannot solve it, he is ridiculed.[10]

  On her first day at work, a bank teller finds an eccentric customer directed to her station who asks questions impossible to answer. The other bank employees know that the customer is odd, and when the teller shows frustration, they laugh uproariously. She feels terrible.

- Foreigners are isolated at first: they may not enter the territory until they have proven their good intentions by making an offering of food.[11]

Bob, a construction worker, is excluded from the after-work beer-drinking sessions for two weeks. He is told there's not enough beer to go around. Finally Bob brings beer for everyone; henceforth he is included in the group.

- After living alone for weeks in a hut outside the village boundaries, having to fend for himself by stealing food, the boy initiate is finally accepted as a member of the tribe.

  After having spent weeks feeling totally isolated, never having her questions answered, not participating in office social functions, and having to find out everything by herself, the new secretary is finally included by her coworkers.

- Young warriors out on their first hunt must wear a special headdress signaling their newness.[12]

  In a California amusement park, new employees wear a yellow tag to display their status.

- Women and nontribal members are never allowed into the men's hut.

  Some men's clubs and social organizations do not allow women to join.

In all of these events, the separation phase is accomplished by singling out the individual by noninclusion in conversation or social event.

INCORPORATION: EARNING YOUR STRIPES; BECOMING A MEMBER

We have many words describing the new person in our midst: novice, apprentice, beginner, boot, colt, fledgling, freshman, neophyte, newcomer, novice, punk, recruit, rookie, tenderfoot, amateur, cub, postulant, probationer, greenhorn, greeny, learner, student, trainee, undergraduate, and debutante. Only when we are no longer new, when we have learned the ropes, paid our dues, and passed muster, can we earn our stripes and finally become one of the team.

In this final stage which anthropologists call incorporation, the stranger is accepted into the tribe, the boy into the society of men,

Table 2.1

STAGES	AMERICAN TERMS	ANTHROPOLOGICAL TERMS	TASKS	NEWCOMER'S POSITION
Exclusion	learn the ropes	Separation	learn the job	Outsider
Undesirable assignments	pay your dues	Separation	learn the culture of organization	Lowest on totem pole
Hazing	pass muster	Transition	allow teasing and testing	On probation
Membership	earn your stripes	Incorporation	produce and perform	Insider
			teach others	Oldtimer

and the girl among the marriageable women, all ceremonies accompanied by great celebration. In our culture, we see analogies in fraternity pledge nights, graduation ceremonies, swearings-in, and inaugurations; all include exhortations by our elders or oaths of loyalty. Still today, at the beginning of each semester one of the authors must sign a loyalty oath before being allowed to teach in the university. In the workplace, our ceremonies of acceptance for the newcomer are less dramatic. We call this stage membership or earning your stripes, which in a way is the arrival place. The person is now not only a member of the group, he or she is an insider. Acceptance is not usually marked by a specific event, but just by the fact of the person's inclusion, whether by an informal get-together after work, by casual sharing of information and gossip, or by the implicit assumption that the newcomer will become an oldtimer and will therefore take part in hazing other newcomers.

Whether called separation, transition, and incorporation, or learning the ropes, paying your dues, passing muster, and earning your stripes, these initiation rites have one great difference. In primitive tribes, the rites of passage are public, the tasks are defined, the candidates know more or less what to expect, the rules of behavior are spelled out, and above all, they know that this rite is common practice, that they are not the first or the only ones subjected to these ordeals. Not so for today's employees newly entering an organization. Now the initiation rites are covert, criteria for membership are unknown, tests are unpredictable, correct behavior is not spelled out, and more often than not the new people believe they are being singled out for harassment because of something they have done wrong or because of some unacceptable trait. If they don't blame themselves for what is happening, they blame their coworkers, and will sometimes quit rather than continue to suffer, ignorant of the causes behind all the pain. Nearly ten percent of the sample we surveyed had quit, and 75 percent said that they experienced hazing as mostly unpleasant and, at times, even painful.

Table 2.1 summarizes the terms we apply to the newcomer's stages, tasks, and activities in changing roles from outsider, through lowest on the totem pole, to insider, and finally to oldtimer.

These stages may be concurrent or sequential. You may be learning the ropes and paying your dues at the same time or one after the other. You are being both teased and tested. In fact, some forms of teasing are part of the testing.

MEN'S HUTS

Brave women are entering
the men's sacred huts
where none have trod before

Some will be eaten by crocodiles
a few will learn the ritual dances
and be accepted by the tribesmen

But outside of the village walls
more women wait
to come in.

Hazing or Harassment?

HOW do you distinguish between harassment and hazing? How can you really know whether you're experiencing the normal rites of passage — the usual type of hazing that other newcomers go through — or whether you are being harassed, with only a slim chance of ever being accepted no matter what you do?

To distinguish hazing from harassment, we have devised criteria for events that can be defined as hazing:

1. It is done to most new employees.
2. There is a similarity as to the type of hazing.
3. It stops if the new persons react acceptably (they go along with the teasing, do not report it to the boss, do not get angry or upset, learn the needed skills, defer to the senior people).
4. The new people eventually become part of the group and are either told about the practices as other newcomers arrive or understand the purpose in what they have gone through.
5. To firmly establish their recent inclusion in the group, they will perpetuate the system by hazing others.

Sexual harassment, as defined under the Equal Employment Opportunity Act, can give us insight into the nature of harassment in general:

> Unwelcome sexual advances, requests for sexual favors, and other verbal and/or physical conduct of a sexual nature. Submission to such conduct is made either explicitly or implicitly a term or condition of an individual's employment; submission to or rejection of such conduct by an individual is used as the basis for employment decisions affecting such individual; or such conduct has the purpose or effect of unreasonably interfering with an individual's work performance or creating an intimidating, hostile, or offensive working environment.

Most of our examples can be considered hazing because they are typical of the experience imposed on newcomers and the outcome is acceptance by the group. Many of the people we interviewed who had quit their jobs because of hazing said that they would *not* have quit had they known what to expect. The importance of knowing the difference between hazing and harassment is illustrated in these examples:

Mary, a new senior engineer, was locked in a steel shed for twenty minutes. She kept cool, for she had been warned by friends that it was a tradition to "lock up the new inspector for a bit." She is certain that her reaction would have been quite different had she not been told of the hazing and expected it.

In another case, a young woman reporter could easily have thought that she was being harassed, but luckily she realized that she was not being singled out, and that membership would be forthcoming if only she could hang in there. Some victims, like this woman, are aware of being hazed and accurately describe the events as hazing:

I can remember when I went in to cover police for the newspaper. There definitely was a social order that I was excluded from. But now I realize that a lot of men were excluded from it, too. I was covering civil rights. It never occurred to anybody, of course, to have young women cover the same kinds of things that young men covered. If you went on a paper as a young man, you'd get a rotation around the various beats, but a young woman didn't get that because it would mean that she'd have to go to the masculine provinces: city hall, courts, police, etc.

Well, the first few days over at that place, I was hazed something terrible. But now I realize that young men went through the same hazing process. These grizzly old types who frequent these places send you everywhere except where the people you're covering are supposed to be. The police are in on it, too. You'll go to one place and say, "Is this where they're being booked?" And they'll say, "No, no. You have to go to a room four flights up," or someplace else, the other end of the hall. And you get there and they say, "Oh, no, they're not here, they're down there." And you spend an entire day spinning your wheels and going into a panic because you haven't got your information and your story. Then just at the last minute when you're about to commit hara-kiri, one of the grizzly deans will come over to you and give you the information you need, so you can write your story. I survived. I think I went through it for two, or at the most, three days. For some reason I think my period was rather short. Then it was announced to everyone in earshot that I had passed the test and I was obviously okay and from now on, everybody would knock off the hazing. And it was like that. Everybody in that building suddenly started cooperating with me. I could suddenly operate, and all the barriers were down. Now, they did that with young men too, but it really threw them when I came into that place, because they never thought I'd survive it. They would say things like, "My God, what has this place come to?" that a woman was there. But after that, you could see that they were secretly happy that I had survived it.[1]

WHO GETS HAZED?

Women and members of minority groups are hazed differently from white men. The more the person differs from the majority, the greater the need to test for compatibility and reliability. But even if not *really* singled out, women *feel* singled out because they do not know that it is customary to haze newcomers irrespective of sex, and therefore they *react* to behavior they believe is discrimination. Surprise elicits stronger responses than if we are forewarned; knowing what to expect can lessen the emotional response. A strongly negative reaction to a hazing event will either increase the hazing or stop it, but it will not give the newcomer an opportunity to gain acceptance.

Just as no woman is allowed in the men's hut in the African village, women entering a previously all-male enclave are not welcomed. Men often feel threatened by a woman's invading traditionally male territory and therefore feel compelled to test her. A woman is often pushed to the limit in every possible requirement to see if she can pull her own weight. If she gets upset and makes a fuss, "Well, she's just a typical woman, she wants a man's job, but can't take the pressure." In all, or almost all male environments, women usually do undergo more hazing than men, and at times the hazing borders on harassment. One indicator of harassment is the sexual allusion. Even if the overall effect feels like sexual harassment, if men and women receive the same or similar treatment, they are being hazed. As one of the women we interviewed said, "If a woman can 'ride it out' and be a 'good guy,' if she can take care of herself, ask questions, show interest and learn, and know that this too shall pass, she has a chance of making it."

The following story illustrates events that are *not* hazing, because they were *not* routinely done to male newcomers. The woman was harassed simply because she was a woman. The intent was not to test her, but to get her to quit.

> In an airplane factory I worked in a unit with 150 guys, but the guys tried to get me out of there. They would say jokes and have pictures to get me upset. They didn't like me around because they thought they couldn't have freedom of speech if I was there. So one day I got upset and I said, "Hey listen. I don't care what you say. I've got a job to do and if you want to joke, if you want to say dirty stuff, if you want to put naked ladies in the gear and tool boxes, it's not going to do nothing to me. Because I've got my job and you're not going to make me quit my job if you keep on doing those things."
>
> So I was accepted and I was one of the guys. It was fun. There were a lot of Spanish and white guys and Negro guys; we were all like brothers and sisters. But they didn't like it because after I learned the work, the company started to get me to train newcomers. I guess that was an insult to them. But I kept at it.[2]

We can see how a less determined woman would have given up and quit her job rather than subject herself to such treatment.

We do not mean to suggest, though, that we believe people should allow themselves to be subjected to ill treatment. Because the victims of harassment are mostly women and minorities, these groups must know their rights. Reporting harassment to the supervisor is a first step, for the supervisor or manager is legally responsible for any harassment that goes on in his or her department.

If it is the boss who is doing the harassing, the boss's supervisor must be told about the problem. Discrimination and harassment suits are costing companies too much to be taken lightly. Most large corporations have Equal Employment Opportunity (EEO) officers or Affirmative Action officers, or at least a personnel department that can receive complaints. These services should be used when any employee is being harassed or discriminated against in any way.

Most men get their ideas about women from mothers, sisters, wives, girl friends, and from the first women with whom they work. Those first women bear the brunt of a lot of hazing because it is a way for the men to gather information about working women. A woman who knows what she is going to experience will be better able to gain successful entry into the work group in her organization.

SEX DIFFERENCES IN HUMOR

Research on humor documents a number of sex differences in humor that illuminate issues relating to sexual harassment:

> Joking or teasing relationships are common among friends and co-workers, and also these joking relationships are particularly characteristic of all-male groups. Perhaps because males are constrained from revealing personal information that could make them vulnerable, their expressive culture revolves around the display of emotions through humor much more often than is true among women. This could explain why females in such work settings experience more sexual harassment than in predominantly female work units.[3]

Another study[4] analyzed 1,500 jokes told by college students. "It was found that male joke-telling was more assertive and that men told more racial, obscene, ethnic and religious jokes than women. They told more jokes in public settings than women, to larger audiences, and much more frequently than women did, and male joke telling was competitive, while female joke telling often seemed designed to foster intimacy." Given the difference in joke-telling styles, it is obvious that women and men will not easily appreciate each other's jokes.

Sexual joking seems to be a part of a pattern in male dominance that female workers find degrading. Women who complain about sexual joking are told that "if you work in a man's world, you have to play the game or get out."[5]

Generally speaking, there are clear signals when jokes and kidding around are considered unadvisable: "when there is a power difference by rank/position, and when there is a numerical imbalance (gender, race, age) between the group and the individual involved."[6]

There is often a mismatch between intent and perception. A man may not intend to be offensive, but a woman may experience his remarks as embarrassing. The context in which the joking occurs also matters greatly. Some that can be told at a party cannot be repeated at work.

It becomes obvious that we have severe problems in communication if some topics that a lot of men see as funny can strike many women as harassment. We can begin to understand why many women feel that hazing is more stressful than men do.

NONHAZING AS DISCRIMINATION

If a new woman worker is not hazed when new male employees regularly are, she is being discriminated against in a different way, for if going through hazing earns membership, then being protected from it may also spell continued exclusion. Harassment also may be continuous and may mean exclusion; therefore we must find out whether or not other employees were subjected to the same treatment when they were new. An example appeared in a *Wall Street Journal* headline reading:

WOMEN FIREFIGHTERS STILL SPARK RESENTMENT IN STRONGLY MACHO JOB — A BIG TEST: EATING SMOKE

There is even an initiation of sorts in this fraternity. In the old days, the firemen assert, a rookie was given the hose to lead the way into the flames so that the others could take the measure of the man. They contend that Miss Gray is "protected" and was spared this ritual. Indeed, because her job usually is to hook to the pumper truck, she rarely is first into a fire.

"I've never seen her come back from a fire and throw up, the way we sometimes do from smoke inhalation," says Dennis Ratchuk, a 215-pound fireman who once tried out for the Buffalo Bills professional football team. "Just once," he says, "I'd like to see her eat some smoke like the rest of us do and come back here and puke."[7]

In other words, the women who are thus "protected" are not given a chance at being included and gaining membership.

HAZING MINORITIES

Minorities may or may not be hazed. If everyone else is, but they are not, it may be that for them as for women, membership is not possible. Or they may be hazed more severely as any "different" person often is. A person may be seen as different who is much taller or shorter, has an accent, has a different background, or behaves in some unaccustomed way.

> When the *old* racism was at fault (as it often still is), the newly hired black employee was excluded from the socialization process because the whites did not want him to become part of the group. When the *new* racism is at fault, it is because many whites are embarrassed to treat black employees as badly as they are willing to treat whites. Hence another reason that whites get on-the-job training that blacks do not: much of the early training of an employee is intertwined with menial assignments and mild hazing. Blacks who are put through these routines often see themselves as racially abused (and when a black is involved, old-racist responses may well have crept in). But even if the black person is not unhappy about the process, the whites are afraid that he is, and so protect him from it. There are many variations, all having the same effect: blacks are denied an apprenticeship that whites have no way of escaping. Without serving the apprenticeship, there is no way to becoming part of the team.[8]

On the other hand, a United States Court of Appeals (Fifth Circuit) ruled that: "Employee behavior that included raw pranks, crude practical jokes, and oral racial abuse did not amount to harassment sufficient to support a black employee's claim that fellow workers forced him to quit his job on the rig. Few, if any workers on the rig were spared; white as well as black employees were the target of obscene and racially derogatory remarks."[9] Yet other court decisions have ruled that these behaviors are out of line, especially if directed at specific individuals. As we have seen, so long as hazing is done to all newcomers, it is seen as a signal that membership is possible if the newcomer withstands the debasing experiences.

Generally, new employees do not know others and cannot feel as much comfort in aggressive humor, which might otherwise seem funny. Where minorities and women are affected, the ramifications can be especially serious. If an ethnic or racist joke is told without trust or familiarity between two people, it will feel like harassment to the receiver.[10]

Temporary workers are not hazed, because they are not considered for possible membership. It is not expected that they will be included in the informal groupings at work. Out of our sample of twenty-four "temps," only one experienced some hazing. She had come as a temporary, but stayed seventeen months, which, in fact, made her a permanent employee.

We must be cautious, however, not to conclude that lack of hazing is necessarily exclusionary. In almost a quarter of our interviews, people reported experiencing no hazing, never witnessing any, and being easily incorporated into their work group with no special rites of passage. It is not always clear whether this interpretation was accurate, or whether these people either were not observant or were denied painful treatment. On many occasions, when the subjects were probed further, memories of these early events were jogged and people recalled experiences they had not previously thought of as hazing.

HAZING OF THE DOMINANT MAJORITY

Some people, even though they are members of the majority culture, seem to attract extra hazing. Men who were perceived as weak and didn't react to the hazing either good-naturedly or angrily, but suffered in silence, often found that their hazing turned to harassment. Women are sometimes jealous of other women's looks, ability, position, income, or status, and thus may give another woman a rough time until she shows vulnerability, proving that she is in fact "like the rest of us." In courses on group dynamics, we have often witnessed the most successful, skilled, attractive member being dumped on by the others until that member breaks down and either cries or admits to being hurt, which signifies that he or she is human after all. This is an unconscious way of getting a different (in this case, a better member) to conform to the group norms of being not too good, too skilled, or too attractive. It is difficult to relate to and therefore to include a person seen as not vulnerable (better or stronger than ourselves), because perceived invulnerability puts distance between people.

A good relationship with a superior may get a new employee into trouble. In our culture, we have negative names for this behavior, such as apple-polishing and brown-nosing. It starts with ridiculing the child who brings the symbolic apple to the teacher. The feeling is jealousy that one person may have an "in" with someone who has influence.

We don't like deviation from the norm, from the usual; we have little tolerance for individuality even though we claim ours to be the land of the free. Although we say that we value rugged individualism, in fact we do not, especially in groups.

As we saw in Chapter 2, hazing appears to be especially prevalent in occupations isolated from home base, such as logging and maritime occupations, in which workers are separated from the general population for long periods and frequently by great distance. The group members must meet their needs for safety, well-being, socializing, and success through other members of the group. The new worker is the ideal person to use in ways which may be destructive for the individual but which reinforce the group's norms.

Men are usually hazed by other men, and women are hazed by men and can be quite severely hazed by other women, the preferred mode being isolation. When queried about this treatment, both men and women responded that they themselves had been victims of hazing, and so wondered why anyone else should have it easier than they. Our hypothesis is that if acceptance into a group is made easy, it is also devalued; therefore, to keep membership as a privilege instead of a right, it must be "earned." For women, it is especially difficult to get in; therefore they make it equally hard for others. We have seen very few examples of women hazing men except as part of a group joke, and found only one instance of women taking the initiative in hazing a male newcomer. We are not sure about the reason, except that we surmise that women are socialized to defer to men and that hazing a male would not only be counter to the culture but might elicit an aggressive response, which would be a threat coming from a physically stronger male.

In a few instances we found that executives were hazed by their staff, again as part of testing. A college president reported that during the first few weeks of her tenure, her calendar kept getting double-booked. It seemed that the whole office conspired to have her chair a meeting at the same time that dignitaries were scheduled to arrive. Several CEOs also reported that their calendars were double-booked when they first became executives, but it had never occurred to them that this was a form of hazing. In fact, they were being tested for flexibility, good humor, and ability to make decisions quickly.

If, in time, the newcomer still doesn't seem to fit in, then exclusion occurs, either by isolating the individual, rendering him or her invisible for practical purposes, or even by sabotaging his or her work. The result may be firing or simply transfer to another department, where the fit may be better.

REACTIONS TO HAZING

Responses to hazing range from being embarrassed, thinking the whole thing funny, feeling hurt, being angry, becoming outraged, showing the hurt or anger, hiding the distress, pretending not to notice, or pretending to enjoy the hazing. The new teacher, whose students hid a recording device programmed to call for help in a locked closet, was extremely upset because she had been so frightened. After finding the device, she became angry, and the angrier she grew, the more the students laughed. Had she understood that she was being hazed, she would have controlled her emotions and dealt calmly with the students.

The new firefighter who was hung handcuffed, feet bound, upside down on a hose tower ten feet up, and sprayed with a high-pressure nozzle for half an hour was furious, but pretended not to be. The new deputy at a downtown jail was told to get a prisoner named Meoff, Jack. He yelled over the loudspeaker "Jack Meoff" — realizing too late what he was saying. He was embarrassed but could laugh about it. We interviewed hundreds of people on their reactions to being hazed. Here are some of their comments:

"I was humiliated — it is a waste of time and talent."

"It was dumb, but I guess they wanted to know if I could take it."

"Everyone goes through this [hazing], it didn't bother me."

"I felt nervous and wanted to leave."

"I'll get even with the new ones."

"Made me hate my job, the people, everything. I quit."

"It was a good feeling to be over with it and to be one of them. I think it was worth it."

"I'm glad it's over."

"I didn't say anything because I was scared of losing my job."

"I felt harassed and discriminated against. I didn't know it was normal until you interviewed me."

"At first I cried every night when I got home."

"I ignored them, too; don't care about them anyway."

By far the majority of the people who were hazed said they were embarrassed, frustrated, or angry. Very few enjoyed it, but even so most said that they would do the same to others.

The hazing system will certainly continue, and so it behooves us to find better ways of dealing with it. However, there are no easy answers. If the purpose behind hazing is to teach the ropes and inculcate respect for senior workers, relaxed, low-key responses and willingness to learn are the correct behavior. Accepting the humiliation (remember that the anthropological name for hazing incidents is "degradation ceremonies") is important. If hazing is intended to make you "pay your dues," then only time will help. Patience therefore is of the essence. If hazing is designed to make you "pass muster," testing the new person's ability, skill, knowledge, or safety consciousness, then the obvious answer is to perform well and get help if that is the norm — or learn alone if that is the way of proving that you can do the job. If the hazing is meant to test whether the newcomer's personality will fit in with the rest of the group, then the new employee has to accept being the butt of jokes and simply laugh along with the rest. Generally, going along with the hazing seems to be the better way.

If the hazing does take on a nasty tone that may endanger your health, safety, or adequacy of performance, you should confront the hazers and ask them to stop. Complaining to one's boss, on the other hand, is seen as being disloyal to the group. If the newcomer is suffering, however, no other solution may be appropriate. Pretending *total* indifference does not work, because the hazers *expect* a reaction, and robbing them of that pleasure will drive them to invent something else maybe even worse until they get some sort of response.

The most important strategy is to be aware that you are being subjected to hazing, and to try to appreciate it as a way of learning about company norms, culture, and tradition, as well as an opportunity to earn credibility.

HELPING ONESELF WITH THE STRESS DUE TO HAZING

Being a newcomer is difficult enough, but to be subjected to hazing on top of it adds an enormous amount of stress. How to cope with the feelings of anger, frustration, hurt and bewilderment generated by the hazing is an important part of surviving these early weeks at work.

It is critical to get enough sleep as being overtired lowers one's level of tolerance. Sound nutrition is also vital because energy is derived from food sources; eat enough protein and complex carbohydrates. Physical activity reduces stress levels. If the hazing is getting you down, take a walk or do a few stretching exercises in your office if possible. If you know how to meditate, do so. If not, just sit quietly with your eyes closed in a relaxed position for fifteen or twenty minutes concentrating on breathing in and out. Drink a cup of tea or glass of water while thinking to yourself "This too shall pass and I will be okay."

One of the more important strategies in coping with stressful periods is telling a friend or a relative about it. Talking about an unpleasant experience often reduces the trauma associated with it. If you can laugh about the incongruities, the silliness of it all, so much the better. Picture yourself a year from now describing the events you're going through. You'll probably shake your head in disbelief.

Getting a perspective on the hazing by putting it in the context of a rite of passage will help reduce your level of stress.

RESEARCH FINDINGS ON GENDER DIFFERENCES

To find out whether men and women responded differently to hazing, we devised a questionnaire that described hazing as done to Christine, a woman; to Christopher, a man; and to Chris, whose gender was not defined. Our questionnaires were completed by 134 college seniors and graduate students (66 males and 68 females), many of whom we later interviewed in depth. (See Appendix A.) We specifically wanted to know:

1. Do men and women differ in their perceptions of an initiation process?
2. Do men and women react differently to an initiation process?
3. Do men and women respond differently if the initiation victims are male or female?

Students were asked to read a short story about a person's first month of work as a ticket agent for an airline company. The agent in the story goes through incidents that include testing for group loyalty, teasing the new agent by playing practical jokes, social isolation, delegation of routine tasks, and teaching of company regulations in unorthodox ways. The short story is a composite of several actual accounts of hazing incidents. We reviewed more than fifty interviews with people who had experienced an initiation ritual in their jobs as we developed the composite initiation.

After reading the hypothetical story, the subjects were asked to answer open-ended questions about the incidents. They were asked to describe what happened in the story, to speculate on the purpose behind the incidents, to describe what their own reactions to this situation would be, and to theorize about the consequences of their actions.

We derived some interesting findings from our research. We discovered that men and women not only had different perceptions of the reasons for hazing, but had very different responses to it.

Three times as many men as women mentioned power as the overriding reason for the initiation rites. They said that the new person needs to be shown his or her place in the hierarchy and therefore needs to be put down; or the new person threatens the status quo. Perhaps men more often than women see newcomers as a possible threat to their power or position, or perhaps they are just more aware of power politics than women are.

Women, on the other hand, see membership issues as the reason for hazing. Five times as many women as men cited it as the purpose for hazing, mentioning inclusion/exclusion as the real issue that is being dealt with—who will be accepted, who will be kept out. All in all, the women seemed to be much more aware of the relational elements than the men.

When the gender of the victim in the scenario was ambiguous by being identified as "Chris," or when the victim was identified as Christopher, a male, men tended to see power as the issue, that is the intent to put the victim down. Women tended to see membership as the issue, that is the intent to exclude the victim. However, when the gender of the victim in the scenario was indentified as Christine, a female, men tended to see membership as the issue. For women, gender did not make a difference.

These findings lead us to conclude that men feel threatened by newcomers who are male, citing issues of power, whereas they are not similarly threatened by female newcomers. Here the issue is membership, in other words, not "putting down" but "keeping out." The difference is important. "Putting someone down" is a temporary state of affairs. "Keeping someone out" tends to be more permanent and points to the concern about the acceptability of women in work groups.

We could also interpret these findings to mean that if women are not a threat to men, they will be easily included in their group. However, we know from experience that this is rarely the case.

All of the above data is based on male perpetrators with both male and female victims. Our data on female perpetrators with either male or female victims is too scant to be able to draw any conclusions. We know of very few incidents of females hazing males. A typical example is one where the head of an organization is a powerful woman with other women in key positions. When the first man to hold a management position was hired, he was not given the information he needed, was not included in the all-women lunches, and made the butt of jokes at the Christmas party. In situations where women haze other women, we believe men would tend to see power issues involved and women would see membership issues, but further studies would be needed to confirm this hypothesis.

Responses to Hazing

Subjects were asked how they would respond if these incidents had happened to them. In general, subjects chose to ignore, confront, contact a supervisor, laugh along with the perpetrators, or turn the tables and deliver a few practical jokes of their own. Some interesting differences in male and female responses did appear, however. Only 9 percent of the men would tell their supervisors about the incidents, whereas 24 percent of the women would do so. Almost no men or women chose to confront the perpetrators.

Women, however, were more likely to report incidents of hazing to their supervisors or seek out an authority figure to solve the problem for them, thus relinquishing control of the situation rather than relying on their own solutions. Men in the study seldom went to their supervisors first. They found other means for dealing with the incidents, such as ignoring or confronting them. Only when the perpetrators continued their actions for a long time did the men call for help from an authority figure; but telling their immediate supervisors appeared to be a last resort.

Most subjects who specified contacting a supervisor as a course of action were cognizant of the consequences such an action would bring. Nearly all the respondents mentioned that involving a supervisor would cause their coworkers to resent them and possibly create permanent alienation from the group. Yet, they chose this action rather than bear the continued hazing. At this point the hazing process is experienced as harassment by the victim, and a decision to make it end by whatever means, even at the risk of alienating others, is preferred.

In conclusion, our findings show that:

1. Two and a half times as many women as men report hazing to their bosses.
2. Most men perceive initiation rites as issues of power, but most women see initiation rites as issues dealing with relationships.

Further Research

We were able to categorize responses to 236 separate hazing incidents that we gathered over a two-year period:

- 41 percent of the respondents said that they felt anger or frustration or both about being hazed.
- 18 percent said they were indifferent to the experience.
- 18 percent said they thought the hazing was funny.
- 20 percent had a feeling of mastery when the hazing was completed.
- 59 percent felt that they were accepted into the group because they had tolerated the hazing.
- 9 percent quit because of the hazing.

Generally, though no men said the hazing made them want to work harder, many women said it led them to do so in order to gain acceptance. More men than women stood up to their perpetrators. Fewer women than men thought the hazing was funny. More women than men quit. No men, but some women, asked for transfers, wrote letters, or sued.

These findings are significant for newcomers, helping them to better understand their own reactions and tendencies; and for managers, helping them to deal more effectively with their workers' varying responses.

The secret rites of hazing, then, have been exposed. Knowing what to expect will give newcomers a better choice of options in responding to hazing and prepare them to deal with it more effectively.

LANGUAGE

Don't say
"I'm lowering my standards"
but say
"I'm shifting my priorities"

Don't feel
you're "manipulative"
you're being
"strategic"

Don't speak
of your "intuition"
mention
your "hypothesis"

Don't ask
for "help"
request
"a problem-solving session"

Don't answer
"I was just lucky"
tell them
"I worked hard for it"

Don't ever say
"Oh, it was nothing"
say
"Thank you!"

First Contacts

N O W that you know what may be in store for you as you enter a new work situation, what can you do about it? Let us start with first things first — that is, not your first day at work but the impressions that both employer and employee form of each other during the hiring stage. A stressful interview can feel a lot like hazing to an anxious candidate. The first contact between candidate and interviewer or supervisor really counts: it will become one of those initial lasting impressions that will influence our first days and weeks at work.

MAKING THE RIGHT IMPRESSION

First impressions count heavily, and they are formed by all the people the new employee meets, such as interviewers, human-resources staff; potential coworkers or colleagues; immediate supervisor; and higher-level managers. A few simple guidelines will help you prepare for that all-important interview and create a good impression for your prospective employer. Prepare yourself in these three areas by considering these questions:

1. *Know the organization.* Why does it appeal to you? What are its prospects? Some companies and industries are expanding into new markets or increasing their market. This growth will provide more security and opportunity for you. Others are contracting, focusing on a smaller part of the market; this retrenchment may mean hard times are ahead for them and for you.

2. *Know the job.* What would you have to do and what qualities would it take to perform well? What is the organization looking for in an applicant?

3. *Know yourself.* What are you good at and what do you do poorly? What do you like and dislike doing? What are your goals for the near future and for the distant future? In what way is there a good fit among you, the job, and the employer? How will you be able to contribute to the organization?

You will also find it useful to have answers to as many of the following questions as you can. You will not be able to answer all the questions unless you have inside knowledge about the organization. Even if you don't know the answers before you go to the interview, you may ask the interviewer some of these questions, showing your interest in the job and in the organization.

Questions about the organization and its relation to the outside world

- What business is the organization in?
- What are its products and services?
- Are its markets growing, shrinking, or stabilized?
- Who are its competitors, and how strong are they?
- What is the company's reputation in the community and in the business world?

Questions about the organization within

- Does the company have plans for new products and services?
- Does the company's livelihood depend on only one product or one type of service?
- What is the structure of the organization — highly centralized (controlled from a distant headquarters), or decentralized (control is local)?
- What is the management style — tight controls or encouragement of more participation?
- Are schedules flexible or rigid?
- Is employment increasing, decreasing, or steady?
- Is the company's financial situation healthy or shaky?
- Are people promoted by seniority? By merit?
- Does the company prefer hiring from outside or promoting from within?
- What kind of training programs does the company have? Are educational reimbursements available?

- If you are being hired for a high-level job, does the company give significant benefits, such as a company car; membership in professional organizations and local clubs; travel and entertainment expenses?
- Are the values espoused by the company compatible with yours?

Questions for women and minority applicants

- What are the levels of the highest-ranking women and minorities in the organization? How many of them are there?
- Are women and minorities included in the training programs?
- Does the company have an Affirmative Action Officer? An Equal Employment Opportunity Program?

Questions about the job

- What is the job description?
- Where does the job fit within the organization?
- Is this area an important part of the organization now, and will it be equally significant in the future?
- To whom would you report?
- What would you actually have to do?
- How much of the job is mental and how much is physical?
- How stressful is the position, and what kind of stamina is required?
- What are the hours, and does the job have any flexibility in scheduling?
- With whom would you be working within a department, within the company, and outside?
- What are the production and performance expectations?
- What are the expectations of quality?
- What support would you have to get the job done?
- What knowledge and skills are necessary to qualify for the job?

Questions about yourself

- How flexible and adaptable are you?
- How much stamina do you have for mental and physical work?

- How well do you cope with pressure and stress?
- What kinds of environments do you work well in and what kinds bring out the worst in you?
- What knowledge, skills, and experience do you have that are relevant to the job for which you are applying?

Questions about the fit

- Why should the employer want to hire you?
- What makes you a more attractive candidate than other applicants with whom you are competing?
- Do your knowledge, skills, and experience closely match those which are required for the job?

If yes,

- Will your goals for the near future be met by the job and organization?
- Will your long-term goals be met by the job and organization?
- Is there a good fit between the organization's values and your own?

WHERE TO FIND SOME ANSWERS

You will find it useful to rigorously and honestly answer questions about yourself. This forthrightness will also help in speaking candidly with people you trust, asking them to tell you how they see you, and sharing your perceptions of yourself to find out if they see those aspects too. If you have had performance reviews in the past, they can help you draw a clearer picture of yourself. In many cities, college and university extension programs offer short courses on career planning. These courses can give you the tools for assessing your strengths, weaknesses, and preferences, and they can help you set goals. Under any circumstances, you must know yourself in order to find a career that matches your needs and helps you convince an interviewer that you are the person he or she must hire.

Usually you can find information about an organization in a library. The reference librarian will direct you to the most appropriate sources for the information you are looking for. You can find information about most public and some private corporations in such standard reference sources as Dun and Bradstreet, Standard and Poors, and Value Line. For information about the public sector and not-for-profit organizations, consult the many directories available. Then you have the business journals, such as *The Wall Street Journal, Barrons, Forbes, Business Week, Fortune,* and *INC.* Some business-school libraries may have a collection of annual reports, which you also can obtain directly from the public company. You may also find a published history of the company. We recommend that you consult *The 100 Best Companies to Work for in America,* by Levering, Moskowitz, and Katz. This interesting book is full of information, and even if the company you are researching is not described here, you will find some standards to use in judging a prospective employer.

The more you know about a company's history, products, services, and current financial status, the better your position for telling the interviewer why the company appeals to you, and, most specifically, just how you can contribute to its success. The purpose behind this research is to make you a more attractive candidate than your competitors and to improve your chances of finding out what you need to know to decide whether you'll take the job if it is offered to you.

LOOKING RIGHT

Beyond the quality in your experience, education, background, and expertise, your prospective employer will base a first impression on how you look (professional), how you sound (knowledgeable), how you are dressed (appropriately), and how you walk into the room and sit down (confidently). Even your way of shaking hands (firmly) may influence the employer's opinion about you. Appropriate dress for an interview is coat and tie for men, suit and blouse for women. In our experience, hourly workers too are more successful in being hired when they wear business suits. People who interview job applicants prefer to see them dressed in conservative clothes.

Clothes need not be elegant or expensive, but they must be clean and fit well. Even a spot on a shirt may make someone think that your habits are sloppy; a torn hem may give the impression that you are negligent. You may be interviewed by an older person, who may be put off by a thoroughly fashionable although unruly haircut, or by a lot of makeup though it follows the trend. It is safer to look somewhat more conventional unless you are applying for a job that requires an unusual look.

BEHAVING CORRECTLY

Arrive five to ten minutes early for your interview. Be sure you have specific directions for getting to the interview site, and inquire about traffic patterns so that you will not be late for your appointment. Lateness makes a very poor impression.

Take a copy of your résumé with you, even if you have sent one in advance. Have a list of qualifications that specifically fit you to the job for which you're being interviewed. If you feel that you are a good match for the job, say so. If you have questions about the fit, feel free to ask them. It is not enough to say that you have experience with a specific computer software program; instead, comment that your close familiarity with the program will help shorten your start-up time.

People react favorably to applicants who know why they want to work in an organization, and who show enthusiasm and knowledge for the organization, its goals, its services, or its people. Even if you have not done work related to that which a new job might require, you may have experience or have taken a course that might have prepared you. If you are a woman returning to work after years of raising a family, think of all the things you have done as volunteer and homemaker requiring skills that might be applicable to the job you are applying for. You need not stress that these jobs were unpaid, but do demonstrate how these skills can benefit the company. If you were active in the PTA, you can mention that you know how to plan and schedule meetings, set agendas, motivate people to attend, facilitate discussions, deal with conflict (give an example, say, of a dispute that you handled well), make decisions, and follow through with plans.

If you are a manager looking for advancement in a different position or with a different company, then you must demonstrate how helpful you have been to your employer, not only for work you did, but for the results you produced. Instead of saying "I raised money for my organization," you might say, "My fund raising directly resulted in [so many] dollars for my organization." If you can, cite examples of how your knowledge of market research, sales promotion, or negotiation were useful in your past job and could be applicable to the one you're applying for. The more concrete examples you can give demonstrating your skills and accomplishments, relating them to the needs of the job and the company to which you are applying, the greater your chances of being offered the job. A prospective employer is less interested in what you can do than in what you have done that shows improvement or innovation. Your past performance tells them what they can expect from you in the future.

THE RIGHT MENTAL ATTITUDE

There are two ways of approaching the job interview. The mental attitude you assume can directly influence the outcome. If you are frightened and anxious, you will approach the meeting with dread, telling yourself: "Oh my God, I hope they will like me. I hope I look okay. I hope I'll sound convincing. I hope I won't make mistakes. I hope they will give me the job." Or, you can approach the interview with confidence, viewing it as an opportunity to show who you are and what you have done, telling yourself: "They will be lucky to hire me, because I know how good a worker I can be for them." The difference between walking in tentatively, like a supplicant, and walking in confidently, head held high, feeling good about yourself, is expressed in every move you make. Walking in with a smile, extending your hand for a firm handshake, and sitting down comfortably makes an important first impression. Employers prefer to hire workers who feel good about themselves rather than people who are hesitant and have low self-esteem. Your heart may be pounding and your knees may be weak, but sit back in your chair, assume a comfortable position, and take a few deep breaths to help you relax. If appropriate, say something friendly and simple, like: "I had no trouble getting here; the directions were clear." Or "I've really looked forward to this interview." But it may be more appropriate to simply smile pleasantly and wait for the interviewer to start the conversation. Your nervousness usually won't show and even if it does it is not unusual.

HOW TO SURVIVE TOUGH INTERVIEWS

Job interviews are stressful because being judged is an anxiety-producing experience. Some interviews, however, are more stressful than others. If you are prepared to deal with the toughest questions you can imagine, the stress caused by the interview will be that much more manageable. Interviewers want to see how you handle yourself in ambiguous situations.

A common opening statement, "Tell me about yourself," puts you immediately on the spot. Ultimately the interviewer wants to know whether you will fit in, and so you should concentrate on describing your skills that will fit you for the job you're applying for.

Here are some of the interview questions most frequently asked. Practice your answers in front of a mirror, or better yet with a family member or friend.

1. What are your strengths?
    Do not be modest. Talk about your strengths with quiet confidence, and refer to accomplishments as evidence of these strengths.

2. What are your weaknesses?
    Remember that weaknesses can be seen as strengths, such as being a perfectionist or paying too much attention to detail, or staying after hours until the job is done. One thing I have said in interviews is that although I have weaknesses, I can't think of any that would negatively affect my work.

3. Why did you leave your former job?
    Never speak badly about your former teachers, colleagues, bosses, or company, even if you left on bad terms. Talk instead about the uncomfortable fit between your career aspirations and the other company. Loyalty is a vital attribute, and you may be seen as disloyal if you complain about a previous employer.

4. What are your career goals?
    If you cannot be specific about your career aspirations, speak about your desire to do the best possible job.

5. What are your interests outside work?
   It is important to list at least one outside interest, possibly in community affairs. The interviewer is trying to put together as complete a profile as possible in a short time. Your hobbies are a clue to the kind of person you are.

6. Are you applying to other companies?
   If you are applying elsewhere, say so, but do not name the companies. The interviewer will see you as honest — and will see the market for your services as competitive.

7. What salary do you expect?
   The salary question is tricky. Do not answer unless you know how much people at your level are getting and your minimum requirements, so that you will be prepared to accept, decline, or negotiate an offer. Ideally, let the interviewer tell you the salary that is being paid. You can always negotiate up or defer the salary issue until you have a firm offer.

8. How is your previous experience (or education) applicable to the job you are seeking?
   If you have properly prepared yourself, you can speak knowledgeably about how relevant your knowledge or skills are to the company's needs. If you don't know, then just talk about yourself as a hard worker, as loyal and committed.

9. Why should we hire you rather than the other candidates we are interviewing?
   A thoughtful answer is that you do not know the other candidates and cannot tell in which ways you might be superior or even different. You would, though, like the interviewer to be aware of your skills, competencies, and desire to work for the company, and then make that judgment.

10. How fast can you type?
    If you are not applying for a secretarial job, and if you do not wish to use this skill in your job, don't say how fast or how slow you are; rather, ask in what way typing might be relevant to your job.

Some of these are really tough questions. You don't have to answer every one, and you can take a moment to reflect or even to say: "That's an interesting [or important] question. I would prefer to take the time to think about it and write you a note or call you tomorrow," rather than give a glib answer. Also keep in mind that some interviews are meant to be stressful. You could have two or more people shooting questions at you, or you might be seated so that the sun or a glaring light is in your eyes. Situations like these test your ability to assert yourself; be assertive, and ask that only one person ask you a question at a time, and certainly move out of the glare.

Remember that each interview is an opportunity to practice for the next one. I wrote a poem called: "She Who Gets Hired" —

> She who gets hired
> is not necessarily the one
> who knows how to do the job best
> but the one who knows most
> about how to get hired.[1]

WOMEN AND THE INTERVIEW

Women in particular face hard questioning from interviewers. Although the practice is illegal and discriminatory, women applicants are constantly asked about their personal lives. Such prying may be unpleasant to deal with, but women are well advised to prepare answers for the worst questions so that they will not be caught off guard. Here are some suggestions — you might think of better responses:

Q. How old are you?
A. *Do you prefer to hire within a specific age group?*

Q. Are you married?
A. *Are you specifically hiring single or married people?*

Q. Do you have children?
A. *You may be worried about child-care arrangements. Well, you need not be. I am organized even for emergencies.*

Q. If you have children, how do you provide for their care?
A. *I'm committed to a career, and my personal life will not interfere with it.*

Q. If you're not planning to have children, what method of contraception do you use?

A. *What method does your company suggest to its employees?*

Q. Will your husband object if you go on a business trip with male colleagues?

A. *It would not occur to him to object, nor would I if he were to go on a business trip with female colleagues.*

Q. We can't pay you as much as we do the men here, because the guys have families to support and you're single [or married with a husband who can support you].

A. *I'm really glad to hear that you pay according to number of dependents. If I had an old mother to support, as well as a handicapped brother, and several children by a former marriage, would I get a higher salary?*

Q. What are you doing after this interview? Let's have a bite to eat.

A. *I would love to, but I have another appointment [unless you feel it is a legitimate request].*

Q. Can we go out sometime together?

A. *I'm very flattered, but I never mix business with pleasure.*[2]

ASKING QUESTIONS OF THE INTERVIEWER

Important as it is for you to answer the interviewer's questions, it is equally important for you to ask some of your own. Asking specific questions makes it clear that you have given thought to the interview and the prospective job. Depending on the level at which you are being hired, the questions can be anything from, "Does this company have a growing market?" to queries about recent policy decisions that the company may have made on a subject you have been following in the business news.

The saying goes that what you don't know *can't* hurt you. We believe the opposite is true: What you don't know *may* indeed hurt you. The more you know about the company you are applying to, the better prepared you are to make a good impression and a good decision about a possible job offer.

The interview is also an opportunity for candidates to find out how employees are treated in the organization. If the interviewer does the job mechanically, giving information and not inquiring to see how it is received, you may feel that the company does not care about its employees. If the interviewer does not behave well, asks discriminatory questions about your personal life, makes suggestive remarks, or is curt or aggressive, do not respond in kind; remain calm and polite. Correct any false information if necessary, but do not teach the interviewer his or her job by explaining legal or illegal practices unless you don't want the job. You may make it better for the next person, but chances are you won't be hired. Of course, if the interviewer is the person you would be working for, and you can see during the interview that you would not enjoy working with him or her, it may be wise to decide right then not to pursue that job.

DEALING WITH STRESSFUL INTERVIEWS

Most companies do not interview candidates with the purpose of making them feel comfortable in the process. For example, IBM and Procter & Gamble subject their candidates to such a rigorous selection process that the procedure often seems designed to discourage individuals from trying for the job. Their reason is that if the interviewer does not oversell, but talks of the bad side of the job as well as the good, the candidate will see the job realistically and thus have a better sense of the potential fit between him or herself and the organization.

Consider the way Procter & Gamble hires people for entry-level positions in management. The first person who interviews the applicant is drawn not from the human resources department, but from an elite cadre of line managers who have been trained with lectures, videotapes, films, practice interviews, and role playing. These interviewers use what they've learned to probe each applicant for such qualities as the ability to "turn out high volumes of excellent work," to "identify and understand problems," and "to reach thoroughly substantiated and well-reasoned conclusions that lead to action." Initially, each candidate undergoes at least two interviews and takes a test of his general knowledge. If he passes, he's flown to P&G headquarters in Cincinnati, where he goes through a day of one-on-one interviews and a group interview over lunch.

The New York investment banking house of Morgan Stanley encourages people it is thinking of hiring to discuss the demands of the job with their spouses, girlfriends, or boyfriends. New recruits sometimes work 100 hours a week. The firm's managing directors and their wives take promising candidates and their spouses or companions out to dinner to bring home to them what they will face. The point is to help a person who will not be happy within Morgan's culture eliminate himself from consideration for a job there.

This kind of rigorous screening might seem an invitation to hire only people who fit the mold of present employees. In fact, it often *is* hard for companies with strong cultures to accept individuals different from the prevailing type.[3]

As you see, you may think twice about subjecting yourself to such stressful interviewing unless your goal is to work for a prestigious company that draws more applicants than it has open positions for, and therefore can be highly selective. We do not mean to discourage you, but only to warn you about the kinds of experiences you may have to face and help you be better prepared to deal with them.

THE POST-INTERVIEW

If you are uncertain about the kind of impression you are making during the interview, we have a strategy to suggest. Ask the interviewers about their impressions of the interview, whether they have asked all the questions they need to, and say whether you are satisfied with the way it has gone. If **you** are not satisfied, now you have a chance to say, "You know, I don't think I explained as well as I wanted to how useful I believe my skills can be for your company." Take the opportunity to reiterate your strengths. Or if you need more information, this is your chance to say, "I have one more question." In other words, usually you will find a post-interview period when both parties have more or less taken off their hats as interviewer and interviewee, and for the moment are peers talking about the interview just concluded. A brief post-interview discussion will often give you additional information or allow you to correct something that may have gone wrong. The strategy is also good for interviewers, who can ask the candidate, "How did you feel about this interview? Do you think you said everything that you wanted to? Do you have anything else you wish to tell me? Was the interview stressful for you? Did you feel good about it? This post-interview period allows both parties to relax and speak less formally.

When the interview is over and you are told, "We'll call you," try to set a time limit by saying, "If I haven't heard from you in a week, I really would like to call because I have other job offers, but this is the one that interests me most." In this way, you may gain some control over the next contact, if there is to be any. Remember to write a letter following the interview, stressing the positive parts of the interview as you experienced it, and saying how much you would like to work for the organization.

IT ISN'T FAIR!

It is not fair
she wasn't promoted . . .
not because she wasn't good
or smart or effective
but because she wasn't visible
not up front enough
not taking up enough air time

She was loyal and committed,
worked hard and produced
but that wasn't enough

She was quiet
unobtrusive
working behind the scenes
making things happen
helping others shine
but never took the credit
never asked for recognition

And so of course
she wasn't promoted.

First Impressions at Work

CONGRATULATIONS! Obviously you made a good first impression, because you got the job, and clearly the company impressed you, because you want to work there. Now you need to think about that first day on the new job. Unfortunately, you need to be prepared for the lack of preparation that you will find at your new place of employment.

It is amazing how often it happens that a new employee comes in and finds nothing at all ready: no desk, no chair, no working materials. Coworkers and supervisors seem to have to scurry around to make room for the new person. Even if a desk or office is ready, seldom is anything planned for that person. The newcomer is left alone, feeling awkward with little real work to do. For this reason, we suggest that, as the new arrival, you bring a pad of paper and a pen in order to keep a log of everything you notice. At least you will look occupied while you wait for your first assignment. As you wait, you might also ask to see some material — sample forms or promotional brochures — related to your job or to the company.

To reduce your first-day jitters, think about these issues:

- If you are not certain where the company is located and how to reach it from your home, inquire beforehand how to get there and how long the trip may take.
- If your supervisor has not explained the company's policy about lunch breaks, you might bring a sandwich along, just in case.
- Be certain you know the name and location of the person to whom you are to report.
- If you have not seen the setting in which you will be working, and have no idea about what people wear (lab coat, smock, overalls, jacket and tie, skirted suit, pants), it will be

wise to ask ahead of time so as not to feel out of place. The following poem, entitled *Dress For Success,* may help:

> **Nothing too short**
> **Nothing too bright**
> **Nothing too low**
> **Nothing too tight.**

- Prepare your clothes and work materials the night before to avoid that frantic, last-minute search for items you may need.
- Expect to come home exhausted at the end of the day for the first few days. Dinner, housework, or children need to be dealt with ahead of time. Getting family members to cooperate is a task that should be discussed in advance.
- Give your work number to the appropriate people, whether spouse, babysitters, or schools, in case of an emergency. We suggest making or taking no unnecessary personal calls at work, especially during the first few weeks.

THE FIRST DAY: ANXIETY AND AWKWARDNESS

Most of us have experienced discomfort coming into a new environment. We're not sure what to expect, what others will expect of us, how we should behave, or what we should say. Some people are more anxious than others in new situations; some manage nicely, even enjoying the challenge; still others get tongue-tied and feel awkward. First impressions matter, and they last. Coming into a new situation is particularly difficult for people who are shy or believe they make a poor first impression.

It is our experience that women more often than men feel awkward and embarrassed starting out; they also report feeling uncomfortable longer. They are especially likely to experience these feelings when they enter work places in which men predominate. The discomfort is caused by both unfamiliarity and women's stronger need to form relationships. Newcomers can do a number of things to cope with these feelings of awkwardness.

"Look after Foster, will you, Kendall? He's the new kid on the block."

Drawing by Lorenz; © 1987 *The New Yorker Magazine, Inc.*

STRATEGIES FOR COPING WITH THE DISCOMFORT OF NEWNESS

The essential discomfort of being new has to do with not knowing anyone and not having shared any experiences with the people with whom you are working. The first task is to overcome that discomfort by meeting all your coworkers and making a connection with one or two of them.

The easiest way to connect is to scan the office for someone who looks friendly and responds to eye contact with a smile. You might approach that person with a greeting and ask a simple question like, "Do you work in this department?" or "How long have you worked here?" Another strategy is to offer to do something for someone you work next to, or whose office is close to yours. You might offer to get them a cup of coffee, or to make a copy at the copying machine.

Another way to connect is to find the most recent arrival before you and ask how that person dealt with fitting in and how long it took to feel comfortable. That person will remember best what it felt like to be new and is likely to be sympathetic to you and your feelings.

As you see, these strategies involve getting to talk to and know at least one person. It is the first connection that seems so hard, but it must be made as soon as possible because it makes the second and the third connections much easier. The longer you wait, the harder the introductions get. As a newcomer, you are entitled to come up to strangers and start a conversation.

If you're a woman or a person of color working in an environment of men or white people, you are faced with even more of a challenge. It's more difficult to figure out who might be friendly and open to an initial contact. Most people are curious about newcomers, especially if they are of a different sex or ethnic background. Look for people who smile back when you smile, who look relaxed, who look happy and not depressed, and who may be either the same age as you or older.

Whomever you approach, the conscious effort of *doing* something will help alleviate some of those awkward feelings.

PREVENTING POSSIBLE PITFALLS:
SKILLED OBSERVATION

If this is your first job, then your anxiety level will probably be very high because you have no previous experience to guide you. Everything is new, and you are learning everything from scratch. The good news is that you'll never again be in the position of having a first job. Relationships at work are different from relationships with family members, at school, or with friends. At work, you can find prescribed ways of behaving within a specific organizational structure that includes a hierarchy, rules, regulations and norms.

How you talk to your boss, how frequently, which channels you go through on what topics is something you must begin to learn by watching others. How friendly are people with each other? How much contact goes on among your peers? What are the topics of conversation? How much competition or collaboration does there seem to be?

Be especially careful not to join in the gossiping about other employees or your superiors. You don't know who is friendly with whom and how your comments might be quoted. Because you don't yet know how to behave in your new environment, it is best to keep a low profile, ask questions, and observe until you understand how things are done.

If you are an older woman returning to work, you are in much the same predicament as someone in a first job. People, procedures, and values have all changed in the past few years. These many changes affect the climate of the work place, and you may not be able to rely on your experience. You may even need to unlearn some familiar ways in order to fit into your new work setting.

If this job is a lateral move from another department or another company, you will need to use your observational skills to figure out the rules and norms in the new setting. Take nothing for granted; in fact, you may have to shed some notions of how things are done.

If you have been promoted from the ranks, be aware of possible jealousy among your coworkers. Observe anyone who seems to be keeping you at a distance; you may want to approach this person and ask if unresolved issues lie between the two of you. If there is jealousy, it will help to remember that **you** are not the target, but rather that your promotion is the cause of the problem.

If you have been hired from the outside for a management position, find out who it is you are replacing. If the person you are replacing was liked or disliked, it will influence people's perceptions and expectations about you. If the person who left was well liked, you may have a hard time living up to that image. If the predecessor was ineffective, instant miracles may be expected of you. If you are in a newly created position, then you have to invent every step, setting precedents for others. One of the most helpful things you can do for yourself as a newcomer is knowing what to observe. To ease your observations, we have divided the areas to be observed into four categories: the setting (where), the people (who), the task (what), and the norms (how).

THE SETTING

Good observation skills can be learned; they are the key to your survival. From day one, pay attention to your initial impression of your place of work specifically, and of the organization generally. As you walk through the offices, floors, and buildings, you can pick up clues about the corporate culture and organizational climate.

As you observe the type of environment you will be working in, you will know how well your style will fit in. It may be a bustling place with piles of papers on desks, boxes stacked in corners, objects on windowsills, bulging file cabinets, a variety of items tacked onto walls, and people in shirtsleeves running about accompanied by lots of noise. Visualize yourself in this type of environment. How does it feel? Are you comfortable or does it make you anxious?

Or perhaps your new work setting is a calm place where everything seems to be in order and where people talk softly and perhaps somewhat formally. Visualize yourself in this environment. Do you feel comfortable or uncomfortable?

Notice where the top executive's office is; is it set apart from the others, or in the middle of the action? Is a secretary guarding the door? If the office is set apart, the executive may prefer to maintain distance from the employees; it is likely that the rest of the people behave formally, with everyone going through channels.

Do you notice that the staff likes to congregate around a water cooler or a coffee machine, in the cafeteria or a rest room? This impression will give you an idea about opportunities to meet with others informally. Do you see people chatting in each other's offices, or is everyone sitting at his or her own desk? You will know right away whether dropping in for a chat is acceptable or not. Open office doors are a sign of availability. Can conversations be easily overheard or are people separated by soundproof partitions? These are indications of the importance employers place on privacy. Which offices are nearest the doors, the toilets, the elevators? The employees whose offices or work stations are closest to the points of greatest traffic will know most about what is going on. These people generally have the most information because people stop to talk to them on their way in or out.

As you attend your first meetings, observe the order and manner of people coming to the meeting. Who comes in first? Who comes in with whom? Who leaves last and with whom? Is there a head place for the person in charge? The person who sits next to that person is probably next in command. Whoever sits directly opposite will get the most eye contact. If the person in charge is right-handed, he or she will look more to their right. If you want to be noticed, sit accordingly. Sitting with your back to a window leaves your features in the shadow and makes you less readable. Sitting near a flip chart or blackboard makes you a natural for writing on them. Positioning yourself by the door or near a phone can make you a messenger for notes being passed on. If you are in a low position of power, this placement will give you a little visibility. You will be noticed doing something, which is better than not being noticed at all. At least you will be seen as helpful. After a while, move away from the door or the coffee pot so that you're not always seen as a person who provides services to others.

Territory is important because the amount of physical space allocated to individuals is usually directly proportional to their power and influence. The larger the territory, the more important the person.

THE PEOPLE

Now that you have observed how space is used in your place of work, observe the people in that space. What do they wear? Do managers dress differently from executives; from their subordinates? Notice details of clothing: what shirt colors, types of ties, shoes, suits, blouses, or dresses are worn?

Who talks to whom? Who initiates conversations? Who has eye contact with whom? Who defers to whom? Who interrupts whom and takes up more air time? Again it is more often top down.

Notice how people touch in the office. The people with more power will usually first touch those in subordinate positions: they initiate the physical contacts. The touching may consist of a pat on the arm or back, a squeeze of another's shoulder, a punch in the arm, a slap on the knee, an arm around someone's shoulders, or a squeeze of the hand.

Notice these gestures and you will learn who has more power. Observe who has lunch with whom. Who goes behind closed doors with whom and for how long? Who leaves with whom and how often? Who drives to work with whom? Observing these interactions will give you an indication about who is friendly with whom.

THE TASK

The task is the work that needs to be done. Observe not only what you are responsible for, but what others are responsible for. Do they perform well? Above or below expectations? If below, who knows it and are they vulnerable to being found out? If above, who knows it and does it make them candidates for promotions?

Who are the people who seem to control the resources that make the tasks possible? Resources can be information (competing products, pending legislation, having to rush with a product) or equipment (new machines, more space), or money (allocation of funds for projects, travel expenses), or people (hiring more staff, using consultants).

How does your task fit into the general scheme? Do you need input from someone else? Does the way in which you perform your job affect someone else? Do you perceive standards of quality or timeliness that are to be met? The way in which your task relates to those of others will tell you who your allies should be. You need to get to know the people who have the resources you need or may eventually want, as well as to be aware of who depends on you.

The importance of your task to the rest of the department, and to the organization, makes a difference. The more critical your task, the more people depend on you, the more resources you're in charge of, the more likely it is that you will be integrated quickly into the organization. Logic, however, may not prevail. Sometimes people behave in ways that actually hurt themselves and the organization. They are willing to let performance suffer rather than change their way of doing things. New people must observe beyond the obvious, looking for the subtle clues in order to truly understand what is going on and to judge whether they are beginning to fit in.

THE NORMS

Norms are part of the organizational culture. Culture includes the structure of the organization, its hierarchical system, its way of rewarding employees (pay, benefits, bonuses, recognition ceremonies). It is a way of thinking about problems, a way of behaving at work; it is a value system. "The culture of an organization has to do with a set of behaviors evolved over time, governing the people at work."[1] Statements describing different corporate cultures look like these: "As long as you do your work and mind your own business, you'll do fine," or "Always agreeing with your superior is the name of this game," or "We're a family here, and you can always count on someone to help you out."

New employees need all the information about the organization's culture that they can gather. One of the norms in most places of work is not speaking about norms. We believe that this attitude is detrimental to the adjustment of new people. Norms are not written down anywhere, yet are known by all but new arrivals. Often they beome so ingrained that they are not only unspoken, but also unconscious.

An unwritten regulation in many organizations is that you may eat lunch only with the people you work with. In many cafeterias we find that coworkers and peers seem to congregate together, and there are relatively few interdepartmental exchanges at lunch. This custom, then, could be considered a norm: People from this unit always eat together. If a company were to encourage employees to meet with people from other departments and have lunch together, and the people complied, another norm would be set. Another norm could be that, even though the work day ends at 5:00 P.M., most people seem to stay longer, and it is acceptable if employees come in a little later as long as they put in the hours and perform the work. The norm becomes a regulation if employees are expected to be at work by a specific time and to leave at a specific time. Breaks can be from 10 o'clock to 10:15 in some places, and fifteen minutes at any time during the morning in some others. Newcomers must be told about both regulations and norms so that they can understand the culture and behave accordingly.

In one company it was customary for workers to put in a couple of dollars weekly for coffee and doughnuts. One new arrival who neither drank coffee nor ate doughnuts and refused to put in his money was immediately labeled uncooperative and unfriendly. He could have put in the two dollars, requested a different drink, and been accepted as one of the group. Such minor incidents starting out in a job later influence people's way of perceiving each other. That man was never accepted, for the minor incident came to be viewed as a character trait. To be a good member in a group means respecting the norms. One who does not conform is a norm-breaker, a maverick. In some organizations a maverick may be tolerated, but in others that person is ostracized.

Norms are behavioral expressions of the organization's values. Values are not only what people say they believe in; they are what they do. A norm might be that parking spaces are available on a first come, first serve basis. The underlying value system consists of people being treated as equals in a corporate culture that is democratic. If a norm specifies that one is to "look busy" at all times, the value system implies that image counts more than performance. The culture imposes loose controls.

Let us look at norms we have found operating in many companies. These are listed with their opposites to show that you cannot take them for granted: you have to observe people in action to identify the norms.

- People all dress similarly/individualistically.
- People are treated formally/informally.
- Desks are clean/cluttered.
- Doors to offices are left open/closed.
- People habitually arrive on time/late.
- People leave on time/stay late.
- The telephone is used for personal calls/for business only.
- People always stick together/seek to meet new people.
- People wait to be assigned tasks/are self-starters.
- Promotions are made from within/from outside.
- People write memos/call/see people in person.
- People oversell themselves/are modest.

- People openly discuss salary or personal matters/never talk about it.
- People question authority/always accept decisions made by superiors.
- People go through channels/communicate directly.
- People check with the boss first/assume approval.
- Profanity and joking are accepted/frowned upon.
- People collaborate/compete.
- People are patient/pushy.
- People ask for help/figure out the problem on their own.
- People confront conflicts/sweep them under the rug.
- People take on more responsibility than assigned/just do their own work.
- Women are not accepted at men's informal gatherings/are welcomed.
- Women are discounted/are treated as equals.
- Women are not promoted beyond first-line managerial positions/are in top executive positions.[2]

We found other norms as well:

- The person who drinks the last cup of coffee must make the next pot.
- You call people by their first names up to a clearly defined level; after that, use last names only.
- When someone is promoted, he or she brings in doughnuts.
- Everyone pitches in for birthday cakes.
- Partying is done on company time.
- You're supposed to attend all department functions.
- You're expected to stay late to show commitment.

As you see, some of these practices may be functional for the individual, but not the company (birthday parties on company time) or functional for the company, but not the individual (staying late). All that matters is that they exist, and as a newcomer you must become aware of them.

Because observation is the critical component in learning to fit in, recognizing what to observe and how to observe are skills you need to perfect.

INTUITION AS A JOB SKILL

It is not enough simply to observe. What you observe must make sense, and must fit in with your experiences of the past. Being a good observer is only part of a larger skill called intuition. You can use your intuition to help you figure out what is really going on, what wrong moves need to be avoided, and what right ones need to be pursued.

Think of the difference between knowledge and knowing. Knowledge is fact; it is painstakingly learned by listening, reading, studying. It is public and accessible. It can be checked and verified. Knowing is a private experience that often can't be explained to others. This kind of knowing is called *intuition*. Women talk about intuition or listening to their instincts; men talk about following a hunch; they mean the same type of knowing. Using appropriate words is vital. To explain a business decision, instead of saying, "This solution just *feels* right to me," which is often discounted, try: "My hypothesis is . . .," or "Based on my experience, I predict . . .," or "All the evidence seems to indicate that. . . ."

Intuition is really an exquisite sensitivity that enables us to pick up patterns and minimal cues, store them for future use, and then act on these observations. If you look at a drawing of a half-circle, you'll probably be able to complete it by mentally seeing a circle. Some people need very little information to get the whole picture; others need practically the whole thing before they can understand. Those who need more pieces to see the whole are amazed and sometimes feel threatened by those who seem to know what's going on or can predict events from what seems like very little information.

What we "know" intuitively can be trusted and used as valid and legitimate information. By understanding the components of our intuitive skills, we can sharpen them so that we can use them more consciously. The three parts of intuition we call the three S's: scanning, storing, and selecting.

SCANNING

We are always scanning our environment. When we enter an unknown place our "antennas" help us to understand the climate, size up the situation, and make a quick decision about the right course of action. People lower on the power scale need to develop good antennas because their survival often depends on knowing the needs, expectations, strengths, and vulnerabilities of the people who have more power and can influence their fate.

Most newcomers are temporarily less powerful, until they have learned the ropes, paid their dues, passed muster and earned their stripes. Many senior and powerful people do not believe that they need to understand the newcomers. We are all familiar with the often poor lines of communication between the people at higher levels and their employees. The people on top do not bother to learn what is going on at lower levels, but the people at the bottom are always talking about the people on top, gathering information and anticipating their needs. Survival depends on becoming a master observer. A good observer pays attention, sees things others don't, and notices patterns where others see only unrelated events.

Scanning also requires us to use interpersonal skills to gather data. In other words, you use your antennas to pick up information that is already out there, but you also elicit it. You talk to people, ask questions, and check your perceptions. Facts that are often called gossip may have a valuable function: providing data. All people in vulnerable positions probably gossip; those of us who are least powerful and feel least secure are likely to develop more sensitive antennas. Our survival at work may depend on our gathering all the information available to us and storing it for future use. Intuition works only if we can *use* such stored information at the appropriate time.

STORING

Many of us have had the experience of being surprised at recalling something we didn't know we knew. The recovered fact may come from a conversation we overheard, an article we read somewhere, or a report we saw, none of which was important at the time, and yet we stored the item. We act on the principle that you never know when information might be useful, and then we remember bits and pieces of information that seem irrelevant to anything current. Then one day, there is that fact, just when we need it. If we learn to scan conscientiously, being aware of our environment and all that's going on around us, then the storing will become automatic.

SELECTING

Noticing the patterns, seeing the connections, making the analogies, and being able to act based on these data form the work of selecting. A good observer will notice that Jane's comments elicit a favorable response and are usually discussed further. Sharp observing will also reveal that Jane has a lot of eye contact with others, and that secretaries seem to get her work out first. These are three seemingly unrelated facts, and yet we could piece them together and conclude that Jane is on her way up. She will probably be a good boss to work for, a desirable sponsor, or at least a helpful colleague on a project. We draw this conclusion because we have scanned for information, stored it, and selected the elements to form an opinion and a prediction. Thus, selection includes picking out the responses that seem appropriate according to the information we have stored.

A new manager in a large company reported that she entered a room where her boss and several members of her staff were waiting for her, and as she walked in, she sensed that something was wrong. She told them so and indeed they admitted a problem had come up that she could address right then and there. When asked what sign she had picked up, at first she couldn't say. As she thought about it, she recalled that though she had been there only a moment, she observed that her boss seemed slightly more serious than usual, a staff member was shifting in his chair, another avoided her eyes, and though still another greeted her warmly, her voice was pitched a bit higher than normal. None of these clues is dramatic or really perceptible unless our antennas are deployed. She had stored the more usual ways in which these people behaved, and so she could spot the difference between their normal ways and the present. Putting all these hints together, she saw a pattern that meant a problem was afoot. Because she was able to sense impending conflict, this manager could act to defuse it immediately.

The manager we have described had several strategies she could choose from. One was to directly confront the problem and say, "I sense a lot of tension. What's going on?" Another approach was to avoid the problem by trying to engage the people in a different topic, redirecting the tension for the time being. Her ability to sense the trouble allowed her to take control. Because she chose to address the problem directly, she was not taken by surprise. Both her boss and her staff saw her as effective because of her skilled intuition. Still she took a risk in confronting the "perceived" problem head-on. She trusted her instincts, and based a decision on the cues she picked up. All this processing took no longer than thirty seconds. As a newcomer, she was taking a risk, but the choice established her reputation as both perceptive and unafraid to deal with conflict.

Another example of an intuitive response that did not work so well was that of a new staff member in a large company. Transferred to the department from another unit, she attended a meeting that dragged on, accomplishing little. She felt that others also must be bored with the meeting. Following her instinct, she spoke out, asking if everyone was satisfied with the way the meeting was progressing, and suggesting that they stop a moment to examine the work still to be done. Although her intuitive feeling was correct, she was too much of a newcomer to confront the departmental norm allowing ineffective meetings to go on. She did not think of herself as new, having worked for the company in other departments for many years, yet she was new to the people in this work group and therefore her action was seen as inappropriate. Had she waited a few weeks and made the same comment, she might have been seen as a risk-taker who could be counted on to cut through inefficiency. In this instance, her bad timing was the culprit.

When you feel that something unusual is going on, consider what information is available, what it is that alerted you, and then decide if the time is right to act on that perception.

ACTING ON YOUR INTUITION IS NOT APPROPRIATE TO ALL SITUATIONS

If a meeting drags on and you *know* that everyone is as bored as you are, but the president of the company is holding forth, it would be poor judgment to ask if everyone is satisfied with the way things are going. The president might take your initiative as a personal attack on him.

Still, one of the hardest tasks is to make a decision when you hold incomplete information. We can seldom, if ever, have enough information to make an entirely foolproof decision. Studies show "that senior managers use intuition in at least five distinct ways: to *sense* when a problem exists, to *perform* well-learned behavior patterns rapidly, to *synthesize* isolated bits of data and experience into an integrated picture, to *check* on results of a more rational analysis, and to *bypass* in-depth analysis and move rapidly to come up with plausible solutions."[3]

Many of us have gut feelings, but are not necessarily gutsy. We know, but do not act on our knowing because it comes from intuition, and we have been taught that decisions should be based only on knowledge, on fact, on logic, on rationality. When all is said and done, though, people who follow their instinct and their intuition, and treat those feelings as data, gathered consciously and unconsciously over a period of time, are the ones who survive best in the complex work environments of today.[4]

FALLING THROUGH THE CRACKS

I'm often not quite ready
to let go of the past
and so not quite ready
to commit to the future

I'm often
so attached to the old
that I'm not willing
to tackle the new

Some situations are not quite
bad enough to leave
but yet not quite
good enough to stay

However, if I sit too long
between two chairs
I'm in greater danger of
falling right through the cracks.

From Outsider to Insider

ENTRY STYLES

We all have our own entry style, a set of behaviors to follow when we're new to a situation. The person who tries to get in too quickly may be seen as pushy. The person who lays back too long may be labeled passive and uninvolved. Whether people in the group are low-key and polite or high-energy and constantly interrupting one another, the newcomer will be seen as fitting or not fitting in. One of the authors tends to be very active when entering a new group; the other is inclined to hold back for a long time before saying anything. The very active person joining a quiet work group would become impatient with the group's low-key style and probably display irritation in such a way as to become unacceptable to the group. The quieter person in the active group may be overlooked and not heard. It is essential for you, the newcomer, to observe the type of environment you are now working in, and analyze your personal style to see where you may fit and where you may need either to push yourself to participate more actively, or to pull back somewhat.

To analyze your personal style, observe yourself in new situations. Recall how you behaved when you were new somewhere. Ask a friend or relative to describe how he or she perceived you recently in a situation where you knew no one. Chances are, they will have observed a pattern that you will repeat. If you feel your approach is functional, then you should continue doing it. If you feel you could improve, then pay attention next time and try different methods of fitting in more quickly.

SIZING UP YOUR NEW BOSS

Your first day should begin with a meeting with your new boss. You first need to find out:

- What you are responsible for (the job).
- Whom you are accountable to (the person).
- What the expectations for you are on that first day and on subsequent days (the task).

Ask your boss how often you are to meet with him or her. Always have an agenda prepared for these meetings. In this way you won't forget something critical.

How do you behave around a boss you don't know? Deferentially! He or she is your superior, whose style you do not know; be cautious, polite, listen carefully, and ask all questions that seem relevant to you. Some bosses will make you feel at ease very quickly, others will make you feel uncomfortable. Try to identify the behaviors that trigger feelings of comfort or discomfort in you. Sometimes, identifying the cause of a negative feeling helps to dissolve it.

Your superior should review with you how you're doing at the end of your first day and frequently after that. He or she might learn from your fresh first impressions, but do not offer them unless you are asked. You can, though, get some questions answered. This review should help the two of you to build a relationship.

Remember that being a newcomer can be an exhausting experience. A lot of energy goes into dealing with your new environment, trying to figure out who is friendly and reliable, who is competent and who is not. You may be unusually tired those first few days, and it may be weeks until you settle in at your place of work. Don't plan too many late evenings out at the beginning, because you will need your sleep.

How will you know when you and your boss have established a good relationship? Does your boss call you in and discuss office matters (probably only in a higher-level job)? Is your boss able to give you feedback and tell you how you are progressing? Are you getting both positive and negative feedback from your boss? How closely does your boss supervise you? Does your boss delegate to you? Some of these issues may have nothing to do with your performance, but may depend on your boss's personality. Some bosses supervise closely, others are more trusting and don't need to look into assignments until they are completed. Learning to work with your type of boss can be easier if you observe how your boss functions not only with you, but with other people. Functioning in the same way with everyone tells you something about his or her personality. If, however, your boss acts differently with you than with others, that reflects the specific relationship you have with him or her.

GETTING TO KNOW YOUR NEW COWORKERS

Make as much contact with coworkers as possible at the beginning while it still is acceptable to ask questions. You will find out very quickly whether your interruptions are welcome or whether they are an irritation. Meet as many people individually as you can and as quickly as possible. Go to your coworkers' offices, sit down, and chat with them about their jobs and concerns. Find out what works for them and what doesn't; what they like and don't like. Find out if people socialize after work. If several groups have their own gatherings, wait to see which one you will be most compatible with. Avoid becoming a member of any group too soon, though. You don't want to join a group that has little clout and lacks respect from the rest of the organization. Take time to study the cliques, and when you feel you have enough information, ask if you can join in a conversation or a luncheon because you would like to get to know them. On the other hand, don't stay away too long, waiting for an invitation; it may never come. Remember, it is usually up to you to initiate.

If you are a woman in a primarily male organization, or a person of color in a mostly white company, trying to become part of informal groupings is doubly necessary. People tend to look for others who are like themselves because they feel most comfortable with them, and they avoid making the effort to get to know someone they perceive as different. The sooner you become known, the sooner you will be able to blend in and feel comfortable yourself. The approach is not easy, but you need to make the effort.

Be careful not to share too much about your personal life too soon. Instead of being first to volunteer information, wait to see how much the others say about themselves. See whether the norm is to talk about one's personal affairs or not. In most places the norm is not to discuss one's salary. Don't tell anyone what you're earning unless you are quite sure it will not create problems for you. The risk is that someone earning less than you will be jealous and complain or will try to make you look bad. Or, if you reveal that your salary is less than others', it might be seen as a sign that you deserve less. You can tell if you are beginning to break the ice with coworkers if they come to talk to you in your office or in your territory and if you are included in the informal networks around the water cooler, at coffee breaks, or at mealtime. When people ask you to join them and you are privy to office gossip and confidential information, you know you are beginning to fit in.

LEARNING ABOUT YOUR NEW SUBORDINATES

If you are a new manager with an inherited work force, you have a different agenda for your first day. High on the list is the need to get to know your subordinates. One way is to ask to see them individually; another is to hold a group meeting just to get acquainted and then see them one by one on subsequent days. Which way you choose will depend on the time available, the number of people who report to you, and what else needs to be done right away.

Learn from your workers about their problems and what they like about their jobs. Make notes on what they tell you because remembering can be tough with so much other information coming your way. In meeting with your subordinates, discuss your own hopes for the organization's future, and share something personal so that they can begin to get a feel for you. These are the moments when first impressions are formed. Think carefully about what impression you want to convey and then find the means to do it.

You will know that you have begun to earn subordinates' trust when they come directly to you for help, ask you for feedback, collaborate by giving you correct information, accept your suggestions, and are generally warm and friendly when you say hello and ask how they are.

FIRST MEETINGS

Your behavior in your first few meetings sets the tone for future relationships. You may wonder whether to speak at the first opportunity so that people will get to know you, or to wait until you better understand what is going on. Speaking out before you know the norm may come across as inappropriate. Remaining silent too long and then finally speaking out may put you under enormous pressure to perform and say something impressive. When you do choose to speak, above all prepare well for the meeting. If you know the agenda, have questions and comments ready. If the agenda is not prepared in advance, listen for any expressions unique to the group and ask to have them explained, especially acronyms or project names. Another tactic we have found useful is to make brief, noncommittal comments early in the meeting, such as "Uh-huh," "I agree," "Interesting," "Could you say more?" or "Would you please clarify?" All of these are legitimate interjections, especially at the beginning of one's tenure when not knowing it all is seen as appropriate and the need to find out praiseworthy. In other words, your voice is heard all along, and when you finally say something more significant it will not be received with: "Finally, the newcomer is saying something!"

Remember that you do something for the first time only once. The second meeting you attend, the second time you meet with your boss, colleagues, or subordinates, is bound to be easier than the first time. With each day that foreign world you entered will be more familiar to you, and others will find you familiar — you will be on the way to "fitting in." We cannot make the time go faster, but we can suggest ways of becoming an accepted member of a group a little sooner.

SURVIVING YOUR FIRST DAYS

Congratulations again! You have survived your first day at work. You have met some of the people, whose names you may quickly have forgotten, you may have gotten lost, and you probably have felt totally at sea. Be patient with yourself — you are going through one of life's major transitions. Whether you have shifted from student to worker, from housewife to worker, from one company to another, from worker to supervisor, from technical position to manager, or from government to industry, dozens of things will be new to you. Among *the changes:*

- job description
- responsibilities
- your expectations
- others' expectations of you
- job title
- reporting relationships
- information needs
- information availability
- commuting patterns
- work space
- language (even though it is still English)
- norms
- code of ethics
- reference group
- technologies
- formal and informal procedures
- reward systems
- type of feedback
- frequency of contact with others
- quality of interaction
- challenge
- autonomy
- accountability
- time schedules
- standards
- discretion over time
- dress
- salary
- status
- professional identity
- coworkers' response to your new identity[1]

This list makes one thing clear: inevitably, life in new surroundings will leave you disoriented at first, confused, perhaps overwhelmed by the mass of new data. As you observe your new setting, the people, the tasks, and the norms, you will have to decide what is significant and worth remembering and what is unimportant. Very often, anything that is new seems strange and does not fit neatly into the jigsaw puzzle of your experiences. Again, be patient. In time it will all make sense.

SURPRISES

It is always jarring to find ourselves in unpredictable circumstances. Even if the situation is pleasant, it is still unexpected, and we need to make it fit into a structure that makes sense to us.[2] Stop a moment and think of a time when you were new in the job: what did you predict would happen in that new setting and with the new people? Were your predictions correct?

If you will be in a new work setting soon or working with new people, briefly write down your predictions about what will happen. These predictions will be conscious, but beneath may lie unconscious expectations: "people will make me feel welcome," or "my work space will be light and airy." You may not even be aware of these expectations, but when you arrive and your office has no windows and no one is there to greet you, you may feel disappointed without fully understanding why.

Here is a diagram that will help clarify the experience you are going through:

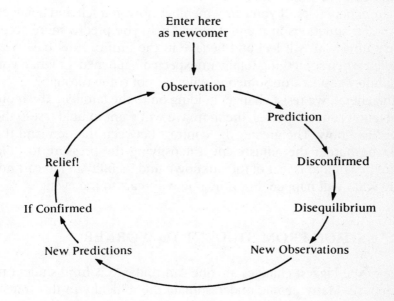

As the diagram demonstrates, disequilibrium occurs if you have predicted an event which doesn't come about or which happens differently than expected. An unanticipated event can also produce disequilibrium as, for example, when a newcomer does not expect to be made the butt of jokes. Some people may be momentarily startled and then go on; others may be so shocked that their hearts start pounding, they blanch and need a long time to recover. Some of these events may seem minor to an outsider, but newcomers are likely to magnify things that touch them, often feeling responsible for their trouble when in fact the cause can be attributed to others or to happenstance. If your boss has been abrupt with you, you may worry that he or she dislikes you and wonder what you did wrong. Someone who has been around longer may know through the grapevine that the boss is upset because of being passed over for an expected promotion and therefore will attribute no personal motives to the abruptness. Newcomers take more to heart when they lack knowledge and therefore see themselves as responsible for the outcome.[3]

Your way of dealing with the unexpected in the past predicts in some measure how you will react in the future. We often repeat the patterns of our experiences. If you can remember how you felt and behaved in similar situations in the past, it will help you predict more accurately how you will feel and behave in the future. How have you reacted when something totally unexpected happened, or when you absolutely counted on someone who did not come through?

In general, we resist change, holding on to the familiar. The more ambiguous our new roles, the more we will want to hold fast to the ones we know. The greater the contrast between the new and the old, the harder the adjustment. Intensifying the pressure to hold onto the familiar is fear of the unknown and inability to forecast not only what will happen, but how one will react to the event.[4]

TRANSITION FROM STUDENT TO WORKER

One of the biggest changes anyone can undergo is from student to employee. Many people underestimate the difficulty in this transition. Students enter new jobs with unrealistic expectations, recalling their student experiences. Inappropriate behavior may follow, with negative consequences for both student and employer. Let us look at some of the ways in which the school environment differs from work, and help the student make better predictions.

As students we have numerous teachers, many of whom we can select, changing some every semester. At work we have only one boss; we generally can't replace or ignore him or her so long as we are employed by the company. A student gets frequent evaluations — grades as well as written comments on assignments. An employee may get no feedback from superiors except for the yearly review. A student learns to work in one- or two-hour class cycles covering several subjects in a short time. Every six weeks or so a holiday or semester break comes along. An employee's schedule is very different with eight hours of work each day, only two weeks of vacation, and a few holidays each year.

As part of their education, students are given opportunities to make decisions on hypothetical situations. Time is collapsed in these problems, and so students learn to expect that changes will be made quickly and easily. Change, however, is not that easy in the work world. Employees often feel underused and are frustrated at the slowness of change and the lack of opportunities to make decisions. As students, we get promoted every year to the next level; promotions in the world of work come every few years at best. As a consequence, employees can lose interest and motivation. It is important for the person changing status from student to worker to realize how substantial these changes are and how little preparation there is for making this transition.

The first year out is a difficult period. In a survey among holders of the M.B.A. degree six months after graduation, 62 percent reported that they were less than happy with job, employer, career progress, or life-style. Only 5 percent of those sampled reported no real problems since graduation.[5]

A no less traumatic change besets workers who go back to school to work toward advanced degrees, take courses to update their knowledge, or retrain for different jobs. Going from an autonomous position at work back to being a dependent student is not easy. Being new in a classroom, especially if you are much older than the other students, can be depressing unless you exercise the wisdom that is said to come with age, which can earn respect and acceptance. Becoming a student while keeping a full-time job can build enormous pressure on a person. Family and personal time can suffer neglect, and a lot of outside support is required to successfully fulfill both roles.

MAKING SENSE OUT OF NONSENSE

A newcomer who encounters unpleasant or frequent surprises that lead to continuous jarring may grow unhappy. In that position you have three choices: (1) leave the job; (2) stay and accept the situation; or (3) renegotiate if the issue has to do with the work, or confront if the issue has to do with a bad relationship.

If leaving is the option you prefer, be open and honest with your boss, for bringing out the facts as you see them may produce changes that will make the job acceptable to you. A last-ditch attempt to save your job is worth the effort. If you decide to stay and say nothing, the consequences for your morale and health can be serious. Working under stressful physical or mental conditions cannot long be tolerated; the price can be high, including chronic fatigue. On the other hand, conditions can improve, and hanging in there may pay off. Each of us must decide how much we can tolerate and for how long.

If you choose to renegotiate the job, its responsibilities, or your supervisor's expectations, list anything that is not working out for you, and make another list of what it is that you want instead. Without a catalog of alternatives, you may appear to be merely complaining, and making your boss responsible for finding a solution. You need to know what you can do to help yourself as well as what your boss can do to make a difference.

If you are unhappy in your new job and are not sure why, consider these possibilities:[6]

Lack of Competence: You may feel that you are not performing as well as others expect you to, that your boss criticizes you more than you can tolerate, and that you don't seem to improve. People often feel this way starting in a new job. You need to find out whether the long learning curve you're on is normal for your type of work. If it is normal, expect your efficiency to be low and your stress high until you have mastered the job.

Not Enjoying the Work: You are good at what you're doing but you dislike the work. Ask yourself whether it is because you're bored, the work is stressful, you have too much to do, or you would rather be in a different line of work altogether. Some people like to use only their hands, others only their minds; some like physical work, others prefer to sit still. In what way is the work not meeting your expectations? Think through whatever is not right for you in your present position.

Not Getting Along With the People: You like the work, you're doing well, but you don't like the people you work with or those you work for. If you have a history of not getting along, the cause may be something you're doing. If not, the people you work with may indeed be unpleasant. Every organization has a few people with irritating personalities. Perhaps you can avoid these people, finding others you can get to know and be friendly with. Sometimes you have no choice but to work with people you dislike. Getting to know them better may help overcome the problem. If not, you will have to decide whether it's worth it to you to stay on.

Different Value Systems: You may be enjoying your work and the people as well, but you dislike the product or disapprove of some company practices. Working in an environment in which you feel no pride can be unpleasant. You may have to decide what is more important to you: the job or being true to your values. During hard economic times, you may have no choice.

Trying to make sense of events happening all around you is one of the more important coping mechanisms you need as a newcomer. Feeling competent, enjoying your work, getting along with people, and being proud of belonging to the organization are essential to fitting in well. Achieving all these goals, however, will take time.

Since individuals will interpret the same event differently, you may find it useful to ask a friend or relative to act as a sounding board to help you understand what is going on. Any action you take as a newcomer implies risk, and so it helps to check how others perceive what you experience. Since there is no method for gradual exposure, as a newcomer you will experience sensory overload: "Too much is going on; I'll never get the hang of this place." You can sometimes get help from an oldtimer who knows the ins and outs of the organization. Usually such people are more than willing to talk about events that seem bewildering to you. You need to find out as soon as possible what behavior is essential, what is taboo, what is appropriate. Expect to make mistakes, because for a while you will still operate under your old frame of reference.[7]

FEELING AT HOME

You're an outsider before and during the interview stage. You become a newcomer on your first day at work, but you can remain an outsider until you have passed probation and become an insider. The transition may take a couple of days in some places, more than a year in others; the average transition time is from four to six months. Some people can, in relative comfort, remain outsiders for years as temporary workers or workers on projects which are in different locations and with different people. You will know you're an insider when you are given broader responsibilities, offered more autonomy, entrusted with privileged information, included in the informal network, and encouraged to represent the organization. When you are sought out for advice and counsel by others, you will know that you are on the way to becoming an oldtimer.[8]

One way of accelerating your transition from newcomer to insider is to ask if you can help orient the next newcomers. Teaching others reinforces one's own socialization. From being a learner you become a teacher. It is a new role and obviously has higher status than that of beginner. Studies show that what people expect from others tends to come true. In other words, trainers seem to get the kind of results they expect. People behave differently when they have high expectations than when their aim is low, and this becomes a self-fulfilling prophecy. Positive behavior elicits positive responses. This information is useful because you, as either newcomer or trainer of other newcomers, can make a difference by expecting to work with good performers.[9] The down side is that if your expectations are too high, they will not be met and disappointment will set in — possibly even anger directed at the people who have disappointed you. Always check your expectations to be sure that they are realistic.

The socialization of newcomers can take different forms. You may prefer the sink-or-swim method, or you might choose gradual adaptation. You may learn better one-on-one than in a group. Even though you may not have any control over the technique, being aware of your preference will help you to adapt to whatever is ahead of you.

BORN YESTERDAY[1]

We have moved
new neighborhood
new job
new friends

We must create a history
so that we can have a past
with every move
we are born yesterday
all over again
with no shared memories

I want to push the time
to bridge the gaps
knowing others
being known by them
I want instant friendship
instant love, care, trust

I want in the new place
all I have lost in the old
without having to earn the stripes
of having to prove
I really am a worthwhile person
nor going through the rites of passage
of hoping to be accepted
and trying to please

I am not sure
I will pick up the cues
understand the humor
be "in"
be "part of"
be "with it"
in the new neighborhood
at the new job
with the new friends.

Relocation

M O S T Americans move an average of four times during their lifetime. Chances are that at some time in your life, you will be the new kid not only on the block, but in the town as well. If in addition to taking on a new job you move to a different city or state, then your feeling of dislocation is intensified. People perform many roles in life, and each role is influenced by all the others, whether child, worker, spouse, parent, or friend. These disturbances in home life can mean that your performance at work can suffer. Likewise, family life may suffer if you are frustrated at work. Because each move means that chaos reigns for a while, we offer some guidance that can help reduce feelings such as loss of control, being overwhelmed, lacking resources, floundering, and suffering depression.

While a single person may sometimes feel terribly lonely, a married person may lose support from a mate if that mate is struggling on his or her own as well. When Monica landed her dream promotion in another town, her husband Norman was very supportive. He was an engineer, confident of finding a job. The day after they arrived in their new town, Monica had to report to work and was immediately overwhelmed with new responsibilities. Norman was left to take care of their three-year-old, look for a house, find a job, and listen to Monica's litany of frustrations every evening as she came home exhausted.

The story is all too familiar. Anyone could predict how upset Norman would become: he would regret the move and blame Monica. In turn, her performance would decline, and the marriage would be on a downward spiral. This scenario is no better when it is the husband who must relocate and the wife who must find a job and a place for herself in the community. And yet this life-change need not be so difficult.

MANAGING THE HOME FRONT

The couples who do best in a move seem to follow these procedures:

1. Both parties discuss the pros and cons of the move, as opposed to one of them enthusiastically announcing the opportunity for a change to the other, leaving no room for doubt or questions.
2. The decision to move is supported by both husband and wife, while including children in the discussion.
3. They talk about possible problems and anxieties, as well as recognize the benefits of the move.
4. Both anticipate how little time the person working will have for the family, which is left to fend for itself in a strange town.
5. Each recognizes that if the spouse works, additional problems may arise, such as not getting the right job, or having sacrificed a career for the partner's sake.

Being prepared for these difficulties makes them easier to face, and makes it possible to talk about them as they occur.

A vital step is acknowledging the adjustment children need to make. They have lost their friends, their familiar surroundings. The new school may have different expectations, and they may have to catch up in some subjects and repeat others. They will need help because they too are newcomers. The skills you learn from this book can be used to help the children fit in a little more easily.

WHEN LEAVING THE FAMILY BEHIND

Sometimes one member of the family, usually the man, must relocate alone, leaving wife and children behind. The usual reasons include finishing the school year, the spouse's job requirements, and the need to find a home for the family before they arrive.

This separation will, of course, increase the sense of loss, alienation, and isolation for all members of the family. The most important source of support in times of stress is the spouse, who, this time, will not be there. There are ways of coping with this kind of separation, to make it a little more bearable.

First, discuss with your spouse everything that needs to happen during your absence. How will you communicate? Frequent phone calls, letters, visits? Sending audio cassettes to each other, or even video tapes of the children will help during prolonged absences.

Another matter that couples frequently do not discuss is the return. How do people reconnect? Talking about expectations is important. Couples handle reunion differently: when he returns from a trip, he wants to look through his mail, but she sits there with a cup of tea, wanting to talk. By the time he's finished sorting his mail, the tea is cold and she's upset that she's not his first priority. Or, he may want to go to bed, but she needs to talk.

> Men need to make love
> before they can share feelings.
> Women must first share feelings
> so that they can make love.[2]

Discussing what each person expects from the other prevents misunderstandings. The person who has been away is not the only one who has something to say; the stay-at-home spouse also needs to talk about what happened during the time apart.

Often when the husband returns, he is overwhelmed not only by the work waiting at the office, but also by the minor disasters that accrued at home. His wife may have been waiting for him to fix the leaky faucet or the door that won't close; the kids want their toys repaired. There are too many phone calls and visits from friends and relatives. There is no time to decompress, take it easy, get a hold of one's self.

Sometimes the wife has filled the absent husband's role and gained new autonomy by learning to do it all herself. She may resent his assuming that he's needed in the same ways as he was before. Children may have suffered from the parental absence, and even though they are delighted to see their father again, they punish him for having gone away by misbehaving.

Even if such difficulties don't surface, being forewarned will help in understanding the family's dynamics. Strange as it may seem, the returning person may find that in some ways he is a newcomer in his own home, and needs to reconnect with each family member.[3]

MANAGING YOURSELF AT WORK

Once relocated, your first question to ask is, "How much can I expect of myself during this period of adjustment?"

1. *Expect your level of performance to be low at first.*

    According to Catalyst, a New York research firm, in the first four months of a new job in a new place, employees had 8.7 days of absence. (Those who had counseling were absent only 3.8 days.) Expect your efficiency to be low.[4] Even after six months on the job, your performance may be only 50 to 70 percent as high as it used to be. A year may pass before you feel you're working as well as before the move. Many people blame themselves — the worst thing they can do. Know that reduced job performance is normal and take on as little work as you can for the moment.

2. *Expect to be exhausted.*

    When everything is new, just coping with what were routine matters at home can demand an enormous amount of energy. Establish some familiar routines. If you used to play a game of squash on Wednesdays, get a new game going on the same day. If you jogged every morning with a friend, find a new partner to jog with. If going to a movie on Friday nights was a habit, continue it. Find your favorite foods and types of restaurants. For a while anyway, the more familiar your activities the easier your adjustment will be.

3. *Expect to be stressed.*

    Lacking history with your new coworkers, you have lost part of your identity. No one knows of your past successes, forcing you to prove yourself all over again. Call your former friends and colleagues often to keep their support. It will take some time to make friends in the new place, just when you need friends more than ever.

4. *Count on a letdown when you least expect it.*

    After the rush of activity in the first few weeks, you may suffer a letdown as you realize everything you have lost. Grieving over loss of the weekly outing with friends or family, the reliable doctors, the familiar smells and sounds, the comfortable house or apartment, shopping at friendly local stores can last up to a year. Be patient with yourself.

MANAGING THE MOVE

If the company is relocating you, find out exactly what it will do for you. The company representative who is managing your move can be helpful about these issues:

1. Will the company pay all expenses for a trip to the new place to check on housing and schools? Will they pay for more than one such trip if necessary?
2. Will the company pay for the movers? Will they move your car?
3. If you can't move in right away, will the company pay for a hotel or other temporary accommodations for your family?
4. Research the cost of living in the new community; you may need to renegotiate your salary.

MANAGING YOURSELF IN THE COMMUNITY

Making a move to a new town is ranked third on the stress scale, just below experiencing the death of a spouse or getting a divorce. While relocating is not easy on the employed spouse, it can be at least as difficult if not more so for the nonemployed spouse, who suffers the same loss of support from family and friends, and the same loss of all things familiar left behind. While the employed person at least has a new routine and people to connect with, the person at home has no one to talk to and no organization to become part of.

Because most often the nonemployed spouse is a woman, we discuss integration within a new community from a woman's point of view. In studying newness, we found that hazing is not restricted to work. Forms of it may occur with every move into a new neighborhood. An employed man or woman enters a structured organization, and the task is to become a member of the work group. A nonworking woman who moves to a new place needs first to find a group to join: bridge club, tennis club, mothers and toddlers group, volunteer organization, or just a group of compatible women whose company she can enjoy. Some communities have organized ways of welcoming newcomers. In many neighborhoods Welcome Wagon volunteers come to the house with a local phone book, useful addresses and references, small gifts, and an invitation to join the newcomer's group that meets once a month.

Most places, however, have no prepared welcome and the newcomer must fend for herself. She may find a church group, athletic club, or a political organization to join, yet she will be the new kid on the block and people will be cautious with her until she has passed probation and become a member. The new person anywhere must *earn* membership. Qualification for acceptance can be defined by a skill such as fund raising, or playing a good game of golf; it can be conferred by "derived status," such as having a husband in a high position or owning an expensive home. It can also be gained by having personal attributes such as education, children, being friendly, or whatever is valued in the neighborhood. To make entry easier, we must not appear too different at first. On a family-oriented block where the women stay home, the employed woman may have a hard time. In a dual-career neighborhood, the at-home mother could be lonely. A single mother may find life more difficult in a place where everyone else is married.

Once in a group, the newcomer must observe the norms. She must learn which topics are discussed, and which ones are never mentioned. Do women talk about their husbands? Do they discuss money matters? Are topics such as politics and literature discussed, or the latest movie, daytime serials, and new recipes? Here are some behavioral norms she needs to understand:

1. When people talk together, do they freely interrupt each other, openly disagree, argue, joke? Or are they polite, waiting their turn to speak, avoiding conflict, and any hint of offending each other?
2. Do they see each other outside the group? Do couples meet for dinner? Do they visit over a morning cup of coffee or an afternoon drink?
3. Are small children kept at home or sent to a playground? Do the mothers take in each other's children, or spend afternoons together with them?

4. What leisure activities do people pursue? Do they shop, jog, play cards, go on picnics, volunteer? Can the newly arrived woman join them?

Wherever you go, some behaviors are accepted, others are not, and the standards vary from group to group. The newcomer should be careful not to:

- impose her own values and beliefs on the group;
- refer to life in her former residence as better;
- pass judgment on the community or any of its members;
- join in the gossip;
- complain about her husband, children, in-laws, or life in general.

She should

- be willing to ask for help and remain open-minded;
- be interested in others, listen to them, show concern;
- be willing to be helpful to others and extend herself.

Even though most people are drawn more to a person with a high energy level rather than to a shy, low-key one, a new person must be careful not to appear overly eager, not to take over conversations or projects. There is a fine line between energetic and dominating personality styles, and the new person must wait to be accepted before initiating ideas. Above all, the latest arrival must show respect for the others and for the way things are. Suggest no innovations until you are one of them.

TYPES OF HAZING A WOMAN MIGHT EXPERIENCE

Following are some experiences women have had when entering a community and suggested ways of responding to them. The responses are listed in order of most to least constructive:

1. Members talk of events or people completely foreign to her.
   She can: ask one member to fill her in; sit quietly; interrupt the

conversation to request information; try to change the topic; pretend she knows what's going on.

2. Some in the group kid her; laugh more at than with her; even talk about her behind her back.

   She can: laugh along with them; kid them back; do nothing; get upset and cry; become angry and confront them with their inhospitable behavior.

3. She is not asked to join them in a social event.

   She can: ask if they mind if she joins in; create a social occasion to which she will invite them; talk to one member about feeling excluded; say nothing and leave.

Very often, both initial entry and the path to acceptance can be made easier by making a connection with one other person with whom you sense some rapport. That person can then pave the way to making connections with others. By focusing on one person first, you can also put more of your energy into building that relationship. In the beginning it is difficult to relate to a lot of people at once. As you build this friendship, you will gradually grow comfortable in the community, and other doors will open.

The important thing to remember is that the new woman in the neighborhood may be welcomed, accepted, and made to feel right at home or she may be treated like a stranger, and made to feel disliked, misunderstood, and not appreciated. If the latter happens, and she feels terribly uncomfortable, she should not assume anything is wrong with her — she's just going through the rites of passage from outsider to group member. She must learn the ropes, pay her dues, pass muster, and earn her stripes, but though she cannot push the clock ahead, eventually she too will be "in."

BEING DIFFERENT

At the bottom of the ladder
if you don't dress as they do
don't act as they do
you're a rule breaker
and you will be punished
for being different.

At the top of the ladder
if you don't dress as they do
don't act as they do
you're a trend setter
and you will be rewarded
for being creative.

The Newcomer and the Permanent Work Group

LET'S say that you've just been hired, promoted, transferred, or demoted. These circumstances seem radically different, yet each one will, in fact, confront you with many similar issues during the following few months. If you've joined a work group that's been in existence for a long time, no matter how likable and competent you are, or how well you know your fellow workers beforehand, your presence will change the system.

THE CASE OF EDDY MARTIN[1]

Eddy Martin, who left his job as manager of a branch bank in a medium-size midwestern city, was a well-liked fellow worker. One of the branch's first employees, he had contributed substantially to its rapid growth, and was frequently called on by other branch managers to help solve their problems. Eddy was also much appreciated by his subordinates, whom he had encouraged to assume responsibilities they had thought beyond their ability. Relationships at the branch were close. There always seemed to be a party going on to celebrate a birthday, a new baby, a marriage, or even a new account won. The atmosphere was family-like, and because turnover was slight, everyone felt as if they had grown up together. Recognized for its high performance, the branch was also known as a good place to work. Buoyed by his success at the bank, Eddy went with high hopes to his new job as director of new business development for a small insurance company. He felt wanted by the company he was joining, whose president, Hal Stephenson, had been courting him for some time. Hal believed that the company had unrealized potential and wanted Eddy to help it grow more rapidly. Knowing that Hal expected to step aside in a few years, Eddy also saw an opportunity to set himself up to take Hal's place.

Because he had been brought in by the president, Eddy was treated with special care by colleagues, who went out of their way to introduce him to the ins and outs of insurance. At first, things seemed to go very well. Eddy did not initiate much, but instead watched, read, allowed himself to be taught, learned fast, and began to get a good grasp of the business. He soon saw how he could significantly influence the company's prospects for growth. Furthermore, he was convinced that he had been hired with the expectation that he could succeed Hal. After two months, he felt the time had come to demonstrate that he had the vision and ability to lead the business to a brighter future. He was ready to assert himself and did so. He challenged the way in which the firm had been doing business, urging major investment in a new line and radical changes in the marketing program. He knew that his recommendations would be unsettling to Robert, a fellow director and oldtimer who was primarily responsible for the company's current way of doing business, but he was so confident his proposals had great merit that he felt sure they would soon be appreciated.

The results were disquieting. Hal became less available and began to relay messages to him through Robert. Others too changed their attitude toward Eddy, becoming brusque and sometimes impatient with his questions. In several staff meetings he was surprised to find himself defending a minority position, supported only by the office manager. His relationship with Rita, the marketing manager, was particularly disappointing. He and Rita had liked each other at the beginning, yet their relationship began to cool. Tensions with everyone in the office mounted steadily thereafter, and by his sixth month Eddy felt isolated. Frustrated and unhappy, he was relieved when he received a generous offer to return to banking as manager of a sizable branch. The career prospects were excellent. Because of his recent experience, Eddy was tempted to leave but reluctant to throw away his investment in establishing himself in an insurance firm that itself was apparently about to take off.

Eddy's confrontations with the president, Robert, and Rita finally cleared the air. He told them about his expectations, which turned out to be unwarranted. They had correctly picked up Eddy's hope to replace Robert as heir apparent, and resented it. Robert was respected and had developed with the business, and the group was not about to see him usurped by a pretentious newcomer, no matter how bright and imaginative he might be. The group saw Eddy's ambition as out of line, and took steps to put him in his place. This reaction accounted for Rita's changed attitude. She had liked Eddy and had looked forward to having his help in marketing, but she was unwilling to encourage him. Like the others, she rejected his recommendations and kept him out in order to cut him down to size.

Coming to grips with the position he would be held to on the management team was painful for Eddy. His disappointment and hurt pride almost pushed him into leaving. He found it difficult to give up his dream of taking over the presidency, at least for now. But Eddy saw opportunities for growing with the firm that were rewarding enough for the time being. Consequently, he committed himself to staying, now that his perception of his place in the organization was more realistic. Subsequently, Eddy's communication with his colleagues improved, and group morale rose because the conflict was successfully resolved. Eddy's ideas were evaluated for their own merit, and the group's performance exceeded anyone's expectations.

To the casual eye, the work group functioned again much as it had before Eddy's arrival. The team survived Eddy's entry, absorbing him into its structure. The sense of continuity made the differences less obvious, although a careful look would have revealed changes in roles, relationships, and ways of making decisions. People now talked more openly with each other, and issues once avoided were confronted as they arose. The hierarchy had affirmed some positions and shifted others, to make room for Eddy. Thus his coming in fact precipitated the group's death and rebirth. It looked a lot like it had before, and yet it was different. In truth, with the newcomer absorbed, it had become a new group.

Each work group has a life and personality of its own. Like individuals, work groups develop, have clearly distinguishable personalities, tend to persist, and resist change. Some groups are happy, some tense, some barely productive; others are congenial but ineffective. Whatever their ways of evolving and whatever their qualities, whether liked or not by their members, work groups acquire reasonably predictable ways of working. Members adapt to their circumstances, and the parts they play in the group are known to all of them.

Newcomers threaten the patterns to which members of an established group have become accustomed. They create discomfort, and the environment will be unsettled until the new persons are accepted and new relationships and work patterns are affirmed. Although a work group will put pressure on anyone new to conform to its expectations, so that it can go on as usual, every new member's entry induces a new life cycle in the history of the group.

This life cycle represents maturation, not only for *new* groups, which go through a predictable succession of steps, but also for permanent groups that absorb new members. Established groups that fail to recognize that they too experience redevelopment when they receive a newcomer often suffer unnecessary distress.

If Eddy's colleagues had anticipated the pressures that his entry precipitated, they might have been able to help him integrate faster, more positively, and with less difficulty. In Eddy's case, the organization was fortunate: everyone muddled through, to a satisfactory outcome. There are many cases which don't work out so well; people like Eddy give up and leave; veterans whom the company values quit feeling betrayed; or the work group reorganizes itself, with uncertain results. Understanding how groups develop when they are new, or how they are reconstituted by changes in membership, helps managers, newcomers, and group members to anticipate events and pressures and to reach and maintain productivity more efficiently.

HOW WORK GROUPS DEVELOP

There are many different kinds of work groups. Some are temporary, created to achieve a purpose; they live until the task is completed. These include project teams, task forces, and committees. Others are permanent parts of an organization, woven into its basic structure. Their life has no anticipated end, continuing until they must change to meet the needs of a changing environment. They include departments, sections, production units, and management teams like the one Eddy was in. In these groups, as in his, performance will be better if everyone works well together, but each member has individual responsibilities for which he or she is held accountable. As a consequence it sometimes appears that each person can work well alone, and the costs of failure to cooperate are not immediately obvious.

A person who holds membership simultaneously in a permanent group and a temporary group is said to be in a _matrix,_ an organizational form popularized by the aerospace industry. In aerospace, professionals in engineering departments emphasizing one function, such as mechanical, electrical, electronic, hydraulic, or propulsion systems are often loaned to a project team created with a goal — say, designing a Boeing 747. Thus these employees have two memberships — one permanent, in the functional home department; the other temporary, in the project group.

The matrix system has been around for a long time. It is common in high-tech companies and organizations that have committees, task forces, and persons in functions like finance, purchasing, and human resources who report to two bosses — their local manager and a manager in the headquarters office. The project team, task force, and committee are work groups with clearly defined membership. Each person in the group is selected to contribute specialized knowledge toward the completion of a specific task. Although relationships within an executive staff are often less well defined, it may be as much of a work group as a project team is, subject to the same principles. Until Eddy adapted and was accepted as a member of the management team, it was unable to work effectively as a group and its performance suffered. For permanent as well as temporary groups, the key to development is output, which depends on how well people work together. All such groups develop in essentially the same way.

Every new work group or established work group that takes in new members goes through a similar process of maturation. But just as an individual can get stuck at some stage of maturation, groups also may fail to make healthy progress. When groups do not mature they, like individuals who are immature, do not realize their potential, remaining less effective than they could be. Fortunately, group development is predictable enough so that established groups can improve their ability to integrate new members and also help prepare the newcomers for entry.

STAGES IN GROUP DEVELOPMENT

Groups develop through these stages, which we call the four C's:

First stage: Connecting (orienting, forming, finding support — *who is in, who is out*).

Second stage: Competing (confronting, controlling, positioning — *who is up, who is down*).

Third stage: Collaborating (accepting, adapting, accommodating — *live and let live*).

Fourth stage: Caring (encouraging, developing, supporting, contributing according to ability and interests — *give and take on one's merits*).

STAGE I: CONNECTING

Persons new to a group must *earn* their membership. Even if you are known to members beforehand, you must "fit in," and no one can be certain exactly how, or even if, your assimilation will be accomplished. That uncertainty guarantees some excitement, anxiety, and hesitant behavior when a new person enters a permanent group.

Discounting or Idealization: Others' Reactions: As shown below, newcomers may be discounted or idealized before they are seen and treated realistically:

People may be discounted because they are seen as knowing too little to be trusted with task-related responsibilities; they are therefore given the more menial tasks. Some people at work undoubtedly are waiting for the newcomer to make a wrong move, watching for a technical error, a poor decision, or an inappropriate comment; any such mistake will be seen as confirming any initial impression of inadequacy. Even if the newcomer works well, the accomplishment may not be noticed or recognized for a long time.

Idealized expectations seem more frequent at the managerial and executive levels. The best example is the honeymoon period briefly experienced by our chiefs of state after inauguration. For a while, they can do no wrong, being given the benefit of the doubt for whatever they say or do. Another victim of unrealistic hopes is the newcomer who is expected to fix all problems immediately. No matter what he or she does, it is perceived as an improvement over old ways.

This idealization inevitably leads to disenchantment, however, for no one can walk long on water. Eventually there is a reassessment and reality sets in. The new manager or executive fails to resolve all the problems, or the new worker does not increase productivity; then the pendulum swings from unrealistic expectations to disappointment at not seeing them fulfilled. The final step is realistic reappraisal of the performance, and the person is accepted, warts and all, or rejected. The realistic judgment is based on the competence, knowledge, and skill that the person brings to the association and fit between the individual's personality and those of the rest of the people in the organization.

The discounting treatment is similar. The negative appraisal is confirmed if the newcomer's personality does not fit or competence is lacking; it is disconfirmed if the person fits in well and seems competent enough to become a productive member. Figures 8A and 8B on the next page show how this process works.

Discounting and idealization lie at the two ends of a continuum. Discounting may not be total, but may be represented by waiting for the newcomer to make a mistake. Idealization, also, may not be complete, but rather seen as a willingness to give the newcomer the benefit of the doubt, a lenient attitude, giving the person time to adjust. At times, neither idealization nor discounting occurs. Between the two poles lies a position that we describe as reality. When new attorneys are hired in a law office, the assumption is that they know enough to perform some of the requisite tasks immediately

Figure 8A.

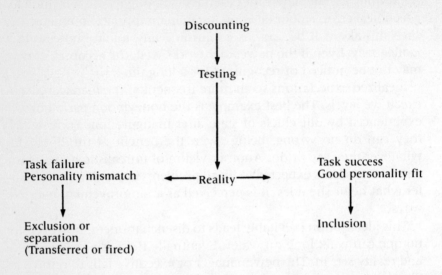

Figure 8B.

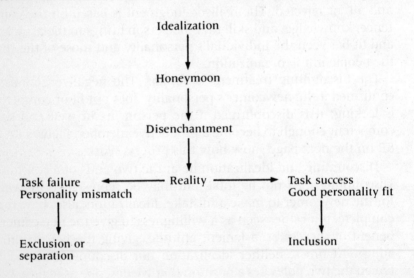

because of the extensive training they have received. An accountant may be handed necessary paperwork, being expected to make the correct entries immediately. In these circumstances, discounting is eventually either confirmed ("We knew she was no good"), or disconfirmed ("Well, who would have thought she'd work out so well — what a pleasant surprise!"). It is important to give the newcomer opportunities to prove his or her ability. Either way, reality eventually sets in, and the person works out or doesn't make it.

The same procedure applies to idealized expectations. After the inevitable disenchantment, a period of reconsidering the subject's qualifications follows, during which expectations are reassessed, by balancing them against actual performance, and again reality sets in.

Both the discounting period and the time for idealized appraisal, with its honeymoon period, can vary depending on the expertise the employee needs to get aboard. The higher the job's level, the longer the period.

For the first weeks and months after one's arrival, one is subjected to continual observation and evaluation, and some form of testing goes on more or less obviously until it becomes clear just how competent, expert, and comfortable one is with the work which needs to be done and for which one has been hired. Either one's performance is acceptable — one meets the group's standards for competence and performs well, or one fails to perform, according to some standard (which is not always well defined).

PERSONALITY FIT

Performance is not enough. Another, subtler test is also constantly being applied: how the newcomer's personality fits in with the group's needs. This is a much less concrete component of the fitting-in process. As a newcomer, you cannot possibly prepare for a test of personality fit, because the required adjustment depends not only on you but on the personalities and norms of the group you're entering. All you can do is observe the people, keep a low profile at the beginning, and try to figure out how you can best fit in without losing your individuality and integrity. Even in the best of circumstances, the adjustment will be a compromise; rarely can one just be oneself, letting the chips fall where they may.

SUBGROUPING

The job of getting to know others and becoming known by them seldom brings the newcomer up against all members of the group at the same time. Rather, we quickly recognize the one or two with whom we initially feel more comfortable. First, we intuitively scan the group for individuals with whom we may be able to connect. Second, it is hard to remember and relate simultaneously to a lot of new people, and so we often respond gratefully to anyone who shows us some sign of approval. Approval, however slight, decreases our anxiety and gives us the courage to reach out to others. The danger lies in clinging too strongly to one attachment, thus excluding others and isolating ourselves. Therefore, subgroupings that form rapidly can facilitate the group's development or inhibit it. If people reach out to others because they feel more secure after they have formed a few relationships, the group will keep on growing. If subgroups harden and individuals stay stuck in them, the group's development will slow or stop. With enough splintering, the group may not even be able to perform at all. Recognizing how significant early support can be, some companies assign a buddy to the newly hired to help them break into a work group. These companies don't rely on chance.

The buddy system is a way of providing the first critical relationship that will, by design rather than chance pave the way for other relationships to form. Strangely enough, we know of no company that assigns buddies to persons who have been transferred, promoted, or demoted, although these transitions are as challenging as being hired. Perhaps companies assume that transferred employees are not new in the same sense as those who are newly hired, and therefore fail to recognize that these people are still newcomers who would greatly benefit from the support naturally supplied by a "buddy."

Therefore, use your time at the beginning to be sure that you understand what the essential work of the group is and how it relates to the organization's objectives. A sure way to get started badly is to make pronouncements on work matters before you know what is going on or before the group is ready to hear your opinions. Timing is crucial: You are likely to be resented if you move too soon — even if you are right — and if you are wrong, you will undermine your credibility. Know that every group has a pecking order. While you set about demonstrating ability, in order to establish your right to be accepted as a worthwhile contributor to achievement of the task, and while you strive to show how people can get along with you, you are also vying for a relative position in the group. If your ambition coincides with the place that the group reserves for you, you will experience a smooth transition to acceptance. If you harbor a hope that the group sees as illegitimate, you will have to fight to support its validity. This is the situation Eddy found himself in. He did as well as could be expected in seeking out information, and was apparently respected for the way he went about it. He was briefed by Hal, read everything available on insurance, reviewed company files and reports, and sought data from his colleagues. He also waited two months before asserting himself. But when he rejected the place in the management-team pecking order that it had reserved for him, and chose instead to challenge Robert for the number-two position behind the president, he was ostracized. Only after he gave up his aspirations were the other members of the team willing to fully accept him and work collaboratively with him.

When a group passes beyond stage I, testing takes a different turn. By then, a reasonable amount of connecting has led members to take one another's measure, and they jostle for influence. When signs of increasing tension appear, as in Eddy's group, it is clear that the group is sliding into the next stage of its development.

STAGE II: COMPETING

The second stage in a group's development is likely to be an emotional one. A lot is at stake. Once rankings are established they will stay set for a long time. One's fate, therefore, is sealed. If the issues are not settled, they will surface again and again, inevitably disruptive. Groups in which fights over power are recycled use their resources inefficiently and create a great deal of dissatisfaction. If ideas are opposed or supported as a result of who proposed them, rather than on their merits, you can be reasonably sure that the group is stuck in stage II, recycling power issues. In groups that are working well, issues such as role, influence, and leadership do not consume the group's energy.

When members are fighting for power, listening tends to be poor. If you feel that your back is to the wall, you will be more interested in looking for holes in your adversary's argument in order to bolster your own rather than in understanding his or hers. This is also a time when subgroups are reinforced. Persons in a fight look for allies and push others into taking sides. Although struggles to resolve second-stage differences are sometimes quite open, and increasingly so as feelings rise, the struggles may be subtle and hard to read. Anticipating such power struggles will prepare you to work for an acceptable resolution so that they do not endlessly recycle.

Resolving power struggles may not be easy. Generally, a constructive outcome is more likely if the real issues are identified, raised, and discussed openly. However, when individuals or factions mistrust each other and are locked in a struggle that both sides believe they can win, they will suppress the truth and oppose any attempt to force them to disclose motives, fears, aspirations, and alliances. Openness will work only when people feel that it will be reciprocated and that they will be better off because of it. People hate to be taken advantage of; it makes them feel foolish and they get angry. But when truth can be faced openly, the resolution of a conflict is often a relief.

Such was the case with Eddy. Until he was able to be open about his difficulties, no one in the group was willing to help him. Only when he realized that he had to choose between leaving and taking his chances on finding out how much support he had in the group could he face the issue squarely. The confrontation forced some unpleasant truths on him, and he still might have quit as a consequence, but he chose to swallow his pride instead and accept the rank in the group that was available to him. Once the hierarchy was settled, the group was able to function well once again.

The second stage is a time for sorting out or putting each member in his or her place. Settling the pecking order doesn't mean, however, that roles and influence don't shift according to need and ability as circumstances change. High-performing groups are flexible and adaptable. It is routine work that requires order, and this is what needs to get settled in groups that mature healthily. Nor does this period have to be a stormy one, full of drama and tense struggle. There will always be testing, applied to both interpersonal qualities and competence, but it may be hardly noticeable and the results may be readily accepted. The casual observer of a group that develops well, with little outward strain, may even protest that the group has skipped this stage; absence of a struggle over influence makes it look that way. The danger of denying that the group went through a period of competition and sorting out is that differences may not have been resolved. A sign of such unfinished business is unexpected and inappropriate behavior, such as intense opposition to a point that doesn't warrant such attention. This strife suggests that people are still competing for position, but covertly.

STAGE III: COLLABORATING

Behavior in groups that have successfully navigated their way through stage II is noticeably relaxed. If a lot of strain was experienced in stage II, as Eddy and his colleagues did, relief is visible when the struggle is over. Energy that was drained away by personal tensions now seems available for accomplishing work. Not only are interpersonal differences settled, but the newcomer's skills are better known and he or she has learned enough about the group's ways to use these skills more appropriately. It is not uncommon to see productivity jump as a consequence. Success supports other developments: harmony is valued, group solidarity grows in importance, and norms that promote it are reinforced.

Norms are simply the unwritten rules that each member must observe to stay in good standing in the group. Groups with a history ordinarily have norms so well established that they are relatively unaffected by a new member's entry. In fact the new member will be pressured to observe the norms, nudged along by colleagues until he or she conforms or is rejected for failure to do so. Sometimes, though, the prevailing norms are changed by the upheaval caused by absorbing a new member, as in Eddy's group. The resolution of the crisis over his ranking in the group led to more openness in confronting differences as soon as they appeared.

For Eddy's team, the evolving norms were constructive, but they aren't always. Norms can be a two-edged sword. They do not automatically develop in a way to contribute constructively to the organization's effectiveness or even to the well-being of individual employees. On the contrary, they can be terribly constraining, impairing the individual's and the organization's ability to achieve their objectives. Newcomers and their managers should be especially aware that norms have the power to push an individual's unique perception toward the majority view.

Solomon Asch set up a laboratory experiment[2] with college students to test a person's ability and willingness to report observations in which he or she alone differed from the observations of the majority. Four people at a time participated in the experiment. Without the fourth person's knowledge, the other three were instructed to report falsely. The uninstructed fourth was asked to report exactly what he or she saw. Four lines were shown to the subjects, one clearly shorter than the others. The three stooges who reported *first* said that all lines were equal in length. Most fourth observers also reported that all lines were of equal length. In contrast, those who were shown the lines as individuals, not as part of a group, reported without exception that the lines were not equal in length.

What happened in the experimental-group setting? The uninstructed persons either consciously altered their reports to conform to the majority's reports, or they lost confidence in their observations, denying them when they heard the majority report. In either event, the individual had been influenced by the group, depriving it of a different, possibly valuable perception, and depriving the person of the opportunity to build confidence in his or her own capacity for observing and judging.

It is difficult for an individual to continue to hold a view against contrary opinions held by a majority. When a person is a newcomer, vulnerable, seeking acceptance and approval, the pressure to cave in and go along with others' perceptions and wishes is just about overwhelming. By being aware and vigilant, newcomers can at least make conscious decisions about the wisdom of going along in order to gain acceptance or holding out in order to be true to themselves and not sacrifice their capacity to make independent judgments. Managers and groups should keep this principle in mind if they want to preserve the opportunity to take advantage of new possibilities that can be generated by a newcomer's fresh perceptions. It is all too easy to take what one is doing for granted. It is more comfortable and less threatening, but taking this easier path deprives one of the chance to learn new things.

Some of the many types of norms, social or task-based, are listed here.

1. **Social Norms**
   - Who takes coffee and lunch breaks together? (hourly with hourly employees; women with women; managers with managers)
   - Length of coffee breaks: (twenty minutes, even though ten minutes is officially set aside)
   - Dress code: (managers wear ties; women wear skirts and dresses, but not slacks)
   - Rituals (participation is required in parties, horseplay, joking, celebrations)
   - Pecking order: (in meetings, wait for high-status person to speak first)

2. **Task Norms**
   - Hours (Work until the task is done rather than by the clock)
   - Information (Readily shared with all who can use it)
   - Expertise (Made available according to need; that is, freely loaned)
   - Productivity (Not to exceed a standard that is set informally)
   - Communication (Only through chain of command; no by-passing or lateral communication. Lots of written memos, even to confirm conversations)
   - Influence (According to ranking in the formal organizational hierarchy)
   - Decision Making (Consultation with persons who will be affected is expected)

As you see, some norms are functional, and others are dysfunctional. Yet whether good or bad, these informal, unwritten rules are the cement holding a group together. Though they reinforce commonalities, the norms may also provide enough security to enable members to begin to express individuality. If the group continues to mature in a healthy progression, members will behave more individually in role, influence, and personal style. In the third stage of development, outsiders may also notice that the group seems to turn inward. Having worked their way successfully through the stage II tensions, members of such groups feel good about themselves and their ability to work together. However, they also become more self-centered. If such a group continues to develop, it will become less self-conscious, and, in time, more willing to work comfortably with other groups in the organization. Then, confidence in their own group's trust and support for themselves as individuals seems to allow members to shift roles within the group according to the task, and to work with persons in other groups according to the organization's needs. Such nonthreatening adaptability and flexibility is characteristic of groups that have matured enough to arrive at stage IV.

STAGE IV: CARING

By the fourth stage in a group's evolution, it has so fully absorbed newcomers that they are no longer differentiated simply by newness. Now the merits of each person's contribution count most. Individual talents and deficiencies are acknowledged, accepted, and taken into account in dividing up labor and allocating roles. Leadership is exercised by persons who best suit particular circumstances, shifting, if useful, when conditions change. Appreciation for services is freely expressed and disagreement is seen as natural, task-related, and subject to rational examination. The group works well together as a team when necessary, or as individuals if appropriate. Because the group is confident about its collective abilities and that each member will ably represent it, relations between this and other parts of the organization are almost always good. Defensiveness within the group is low and it seems minimal in exchanges with outsiders. Table 8.1 shows relatively, not absolutely, how tensions rise and fall over a work group's life.

Tensions never wholly disappear, though, even when a group is operating at its highest potential. In fact, some tension is needed for it inspires creativity. When persons or groups have to reconcile con-

Table 8.1: Stages in Group Development

Stage 1 Connecting	Stage 2 Competing	Stage 3 Collaborating	Stage 4 Caring

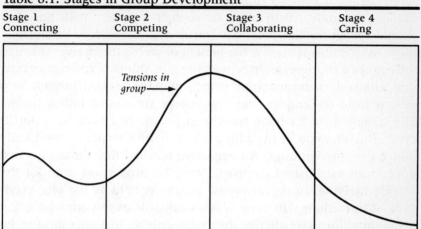

Tensions in group——→

tradictions, they are most likely to be imaginative and productive. Jim Webb, the brilliant first director of NASA, found that diversity in points of view forced his people to examine accepted assumptions, provoking a search for new explanations. He insisted on bringing specialists from many disciplines together to work on problems, rather than building teams of engineers and scientists with the same backgrounds.

In a study during World War II, it was found that the most effective bomber crews were not the ones with most or least tension, but those spurred by moderate tension to be creative in coping with unexpected events. It is a self-evident truth that groups grown complacent or self-satisfied find the lack of challenge ultimately harmful to their productivity. Lacking tension, the group is not stimulated to reexamine its ways of doing things. The arrival of a newcomer often shakes up such groups, introducing new ideas as well. A company prominent in a service industry that ordinarily selects its presidents from its own ranks searched for an outsider to replace the about-to-retire president. The company rightly believed that bringing in an outsider was the best way to retain its innovative edge in an ever more competitive environment.

Newcomers who slip into a group almost unnoticed may do little to disrupt its comfort, but may also deprive the group of an opportunity to learn how to function in new, more imaginative ways. Groups naturally try to bend newcomers to their will, but they should recognize the potential learning that enforced conformity may cost. Groups soon lose the benefit of seeing themselves through the eyes of a stranger, an irrecoverable gift. You may remember how odd, colorful, or bizarre new situations have seemed to you. To a person from the tropics, the first snows are almost indescribable. The same is true for palm trees seen for the first time by a northerner. But after you've lived for a while in the new place, you hardly notice the surroundings. An executive recalled that during his first days in an established company, only he arrived on time for the weekly meetings of departmental managers held by the vice president of operations. His time was as valuable as anyone else's, but being unwilling to challenge the group's norms just after joining, he eased toward later arrival. Fortunately, at one of the meetings the vice president asked for the newcomer's impressions. His observing that no one seemed to bother with punctuality provoked a discussion revealing that everyone had simply taken tardiness for granted for so long that they no longer noticed. Other observations were equally surprising and valuable.

To salvage fresh insights before they are dulled by the passage of time and lost forever, companies should interview newcomers after their first month with the company. The interview may be conducted by the new person's immediate supervisor, by someone in the human-resources department, or by the entire group when everyone is together. The group session is more likely to produce a positive response, because it avoids the appearance of being critical of the group behind the backs of its members. The openness inherent in a group interview also suggests that disclosure is welcome. Such procedures, though, require a healthy group environment that will support taking advantage of and learning from a new member's perceptions. Likewise, the newcomer must have enough interpersonal skill to share his or her observations in a nonthreatening way. The ground rule is to describe these observations, not judge them. Thus, one way of referring to tardiness at meetings is to say: "I was surprised to see that no one comes to this weekly meeting on time, and I wondered when I should arrive. Although I've learned to come fifteen minutes late like most of you, it does make me feel uncomfortable." Contrast that message with: "I was surprised to see that no one comes to this weekly meeting on time, and I thought that you don't have much respect for one another's time. I think it's a bad practice, and should be stopped." As a newcomer, you probably haven't yet earned the right to express yourself strongly on established practices, and if you do speak up, you will probably arouse defensiveness and even retaliation. A better move at the beginning is to simply offer your observations and let the others decide what to do about them.

But even comments such as the ones we just proposed are best received by a group in stage IV. A group at stage II could feel quite threatened by a comment that might be interpreted as critical. In other words, if we understand which stage the work group has reached, we will be better able to evaluate its members' behavior and act and respond appropriately.

STUCK GROUPS

We have briefly considered groups that perform poorly because they have not matured. Stuck in early stages of development, they make inefficient use of their members' abilities and resources. Sometimes such groups seem doomed to be relatively unproductive. People who find themselves in such groups usually yearn to be elsewhere. If stuck groups recognize their difficulty, come to grips with it, and move on, they will become more effective. The conditions conducive to change to a better state are:

- dissatisfaction with current conditions
- recognizing steps that need to be taken to improve the situation
- willingness to take the steps, as individuals and as a group
- knowledge and skills required to take the necessary steps

Generally, a group that is stuck needs help from an outsider to move forward. The members are usually too invested emotionally in their behaviors to let go of them. Even if a group member realizes the issues and the steps that need to be taken, colleagues may not accept such direction. An outsider, perhaps an internal or external consultant, may be needed to help members let go of destructive behaviors. Many organizations have organization-development specialists on their staff who supply team-building services internally. Most management-consulting companies also have specialists who can help groups and organizations build more effective teams. The value of these services is widely recognized; managers who have access to them would be wise to use them when needed.

RISK TAKING

Why is it
that when I make a mistake
it's always entirely my fault
and I blame myself
feeling just awful
for being so stupid

but when I have accomplished
something successfully
I don't take any credit
don't pat myself on the back
Instead I say,
"I was just lucky!"

Significance of Stages in Group Development for Newcomers

ENTERING A GROUP IN STAGE I

The group development principles we have described apply to new groups and to permanent groups that have to adjust to a newcomer's entry. If newcomers are aware that groups go through stages in development as they accommodate to a new arrival, they will be able to behave appropriately. The stage that a group is in when the newcomer appears also makes a difference in the group's response to him or her as it recycles. As a result, entry is easier at some stages of group development than at others, and different entry behaviors are appropriate for different stages of development. If a group is in the early days of stage I (connecting), members are preoccupied with themselves and with the impression they make, sizing others up to see whom they feel closer to, making tentative overtures for connections, and generally proceeding cautiously because the others are not yet predictable. Under these circumstances, the newcomer stands out less because he or she is only a little less known than the colleagues. Although he or she is likely to arouse some curiosity, members of the group are too busy making their own tentative connections to pay much attention to the newcomer. Although as a member you may still feel like an outsider when you join, you have less catching up to do and can move more quickly through this period of transition. By the time the group moves into stage II (competing), you will have had a real chance of being remembered and treated like everyone else in the group. Therefore, entry when the group is in stage I can be less trying than at almost any other time in the group's life.

ENTERING A GROUP IN STAGE II

On the other hand, entry at stage II (competing) is likely to be challenging, confusing, and treacherous. Because members are jockeying for position, sometimes even fighting openly, newcomers may find themselves pressured into taking sides before they are fully aware of all that is at stake. If they fall into that trap, and become too deeply identified with individuals or subgroups, they will almost certainly find it difficult to disentangle themselves later.

Take Peter, for example, who joined an organization fraught with conflict. Two bitterly opposed factions had been struggling for years for control of a department. Whenever a new person arrived, each group immediately sought his or her support. The problem for newcomers was that the struggle for power was covert and not obvious. A hidden agenda lay behind every encounter. Insiders knew what was going on, but not newcomers. Early on Peter found himself maneuvered into an alliance with one of the groups. It started innocently enough with his accepting an invitation to lunch. Peter welcomed the invitation as a friendly gesture and soon found himself a regular member of the luncheon group. Work issues naturally were discussed, and Peter's opinion about them was solicited. Peter wasn't reluctant to express himself; in fact, he was pleased that what he had to say seemed to matter. His reactions were based though, on what he had heard, and invariably he heard only half the story. Unhappily for him, even after he had heard the other side, he found that his luncheon "friends" expected him to stick to the opinions he had expressed in the luncheon meetings. His opinions were taken as commitments by the luncheon group; any reversal was seen as betraying that group's interests. By the time Peter had sorted out the players in the office drama, he was snared. When he did try to break away, he was labeled a traitor. This premature entanglement ultimately cost him his job when the group he left sabotaged him by withholding critical information. His plight is more common than one might think.

Stage II is a difficult one in which to join a group. If you observe that the group you are joining is at this stage, preoccupied with intense competition for power, be careful; proceed cautiously. Avoid early commitments to positions on issues. Look for hidden agendas. Communicate with everyone rather than align yourself with a few people. Watch what happens in meetings, observe who seems to support whom, and how people react to each other, and ask lots of questions. You will eventually have to choose your alliances, but by then your choice will be informed and you'll be less likely to regret your decision.

ENTERING A GROUP IN STAGE III

Entry at stage III (collaborating) may be challenging, but less difficult than at stage II. A stage III group has been around fairly long and is performing adequately. Because of its long history, it has strong norms, an entrenched pecking order, and clearly allocated roles. Pressure on newcomers to conform to expectations is likely to be intense, with established ways, including hazing, for testing the newcomer's compatibility. If you meet expectations and accept your assigned role in the group, your transition will proceed smoothly, as will the group's recycling through the stages in development. If you balk at accepting the assigned role, a stage II struggle may erupt, with uncertain outcome. Norms, pecking order, and roles may be changed or reaffirmed. The struggle can be muted and covert, or intense and open. In any event, wisdom dictates that if you enter a group at this stage you strive to understand where the group is before sticking your neck out. If you are seen as not knowing what you are doing, or acting on incorrect assumptions, you will lose credibility that you will probably never regain. Even if you are right, you will arouse resentment, because others will feel that you did not respect them enough to find out what they knew before you acted. This is a good way to leave yourself without allies, at best, and to gain lasting enemies, at worst.

Appropriate behavior for a newcomer entering a group in stage III is cautious action, careful scanning to understand how things work and what is expected of you, anticipation of testing and hazing, and a good-natured response to it so long as it is not abusive or objectionable. If you aspire to changing the way in which the group works or your place in the hierarchy, and you have been patient, cautious, and observant, you will know what you are up against. You will face a struggle, and you should be prepared for unpleasantness and disappointment. You may win your way, or gain a second chance, but you may also isolate yourself and be forced to leave. If you are willing to do what is expected of you, you will in time be accepted, and the group will recycle without trauma.

ENTERING A GROUP IN STAGE IV

If you are lucky enough to enter a group at stage 4 (caring), you will have a pleasant experience. Because the group is mature, its members are secure, contributions are appreciated on their merits, and you will be welcomed as a source of new ideas. People will be curious about you and will want to get to know you quickly, assuming that you have something worthwhile to offer. Very often groups that are functioning effectively participate in the selection of new members. If they do, you will already be known, and they will have committed themselves to helping you fit in. Groups that have reached stage IV are characterized by much openness and flexibility, and you will do yourself the most good by being forthright from the beginning. You can expect to get help and feedback about your progress. You should solicit assistance, and, above all, not worry about looking foolish. Your competence will be taken for granted, and you will be respected for wanting to know all you can. One company we know has a long tradition in the engineering department of encouraging newcomers to ask questions not usually asked, the ones managers and newcomers are supposed to have answers for but don't.

Although it is easy to move into a group that is just forming (stage I), it is more fun to enter a group at stage IV. The problem you will recognize is that you will not have information in advance about the stage of development your group is in unless someone tells you, and most often, no one does. This identification, then, becomes the responsibility of the manager, or buddy if one is assigned. Of course, to properly advise you, your "guide" must be knowledgeable about how a group develops and recycles with a newcomer's entry. For the manager who knows how and is willing to take the time to coach a newcomer, this is a grand opportunity to accelerate a new member's constructive integration into the group, and the group's healthy adjustment to the individual.

Most managers, however, are unaware of the ways in which groups develop, and most members are unable to identify the stage their own group is in. Thus the newcomer must help himself or herself by asking questions of the boss, a buddy, or the peers, which will allow him or her to estimate where the group is with reasonable accuracy. Think of the information you would need to decide what stage the group is in. Here are some questions to ask that will elicit such information:

- How long has the group been together?
- How long has each person been in it?
- How well do people know each other?
- How well does everyone get along?
- Whom do people seem to listen to most in meetings?
- Who generally has most influence in the group?
- Whom do people go to when they need help on a problem — with the boss, with each other?
- To whom does the boss go when he or she wants something done by the group?
- Who has the most difficulty with each other?
- Do differences between people get resolved or do they fester?
- How are differences between people resolved? By avoidance? By logic? By fighting? Covertly? Openly?
- How do people feel after they've settled differences? Good? Bitter?
- Do pairs or smaller groups within the large group stick together?
- If such groups have formed, do they stick together when they run into differences, or do they split according to their independent opinions?
- What has been expected of newcomers in the past?

Asking all these questions at once, or right at the beginning, or of any one person will not be productive. You have to be discreet and pick up information gradually. Often you can do so in casual conversation. You should also gather data from your own observations. Having a frame of reference to work with, such as realizing that groups do develop by stages, you will be able to piece together a reasonably accurate picture of your own. The following chart will provide you with a road map for guidance, and you will have greater control over your fate in the group.

Table 9.1 summarizes the situations you can expect to find when

Table 9.1: Stages in Group Development

ENTRY OF NEWCOMER AT STAGE I: "CONNECTING"

Critical Issue:	Who is in? Who is out? Becoming a member.
Interactions:	Self-consciousness. Preoccupation with self. Reaching out. Forming subgroups.
Status of Norms:	Not yet informed. Influenceable. Early signs of emergence may be noticeable.
Reactions to Newcomer:	Indifference to mild curiosity. Impressed by outside status and credentials. Reinforcement of early tentative connections.
Appropriate Newcomer Behavior:	Earlier assertiveness than when entry made at later stages. Self-disclosure early so that others can recognize value of potential contribution to group's purposes. Scan for connections that feel good. Take first step because each person is preoccupied with impressions he or she is making on others. Take initiative in reaching out and expect appreciation, because others too are seeking acceptance and approval.
Ease of Entry for Newcomer:	Fairly easy. Good opportunity to move in, fit in, get aboard early if willing to be moderately assertive.

ENTRY OF NEWCOMER AT STAGE II, "COMPETING"

Critical Issue:	Who is up? Who is down? Settling status.
Interactions:	Tense. Competing for influence rather than merits of ideas. Putdowns rather than support. Scapegoating. Piling on.
Status of Norms:	Unsettled and will be affected by resolution of power struggle. Ways in which differences are resolved will in themselves set norms. Contenders for highest ranking in group strongly influence norms that are forming.
Reactions to Newcomer:	Suspicion. Resentment unless accepting of low ranking. Testing for abilities and skills, both task and interpersonal. Measuring against self. Aggressive response to assertiveness.
Appropriate Newcomer Behavior:	Caution. Scanning for status of conflict. Avoidance of commitment to too-early connections and alliances. Alertness to being used for support that will alienate others and make them powerful enemies. Sensitivity to hidden agendas. Assert self by referring to the merits of ideas and not to persons.

Table 9.1: Stages in Group Development, *continued*

ENTRY OF NEWCOMER AT STAGE II, "COMPETING"

Ease of Entry for Newcomer:	Most difficult of the stages. Confusing. Easy to become co-opted.

ENTRY OF NEWCOMER AT STAGE III, "COLLABORATING"

Critical Issue:	Live and let live. Maintaining relationships that get the task done.
Interactions:	Determined by norms. Influence and roles are settled. Behavior is predictable; therefore, comfort level is high. Trust is moderate. Degree of openness is regulated by norms. Individual freedom is limited by norms. Sanctions available to apply to individuals who violate norms.
Status of Norms:	Well established. Observable — can be recognized by looking for consistency in behavior. Reasonably easy to recognize if alert.
Reactions to Newcomer:	Testing for compatibility of both personality and task. Pressure — to conform to norms and to accept place in pecking order reserved for newcomers.
Appropriate Newcomer Behavior:	Caution. Scanning for norms. Acceptance of testing and of norms if they are consistent with personal values and aspirations. If not acceptable, wait to see if norms are influenceable and aspirations realizable. If neither, plan to get out. Do not assert self too soon. Meet expectations, set by norms, of when to start taking initiative.
Ease of Entry for Newcomer:	Not difficult if norms are congruent with newcomer's values and aspirations. But entry takes ability to scan, pick up patterns of behavior, recognize norms, tolerate testing, accept ranking, and assert self at right time.

ENTRY OF NEWCOMER AT STAGE IV, "CARING"

Critical Issue:	Give and take. Maintenance of high performance and ability of individuals and group to continue to develop problem-solving skills.
Interactions:	Spontaneity. Flexibility. Sharing ideas and feedback freely. Adaptability to changing circumstances. High trust. Openness. Influence through contribution to the task.
Status of Norms:	Established. Emphasis on trust, openness, candor, feedback, learning, appreciation of new ideas and different perspectives.

Table 9.1: Stages in Group Development, *continued*

ENTRY OF NEWCOMER AT STAGE IV, "CARING"

Reactions to Newcomer:	Interest. Curiosity. Excitement as source of new ideas and fresh perspectives. Testing for compatibility, both interpersonal and task. Desire to share information and receive feedback. Effort to make solid connections and bring aboard quickly if testing demonstrates compatibility.
Appropriate Newcomer Behavior:	Scanning to understand open environment. Acceptance of open environment. Open, candid responses to experience. Openness to feedback, with willingness to correct behavior accordingly. Willingness to give feedback.
Ease of Entry for Newcomer:	Easy, if newcomer's values and aspirations are compatible with the group's needs.

you enter a group as a newcomer at any stage of development. They also identify the behavior that would be appropriate at each of those stages.

SPECIAL CASES

Sometimes it is not enough to know that groups go through a development cycle and that you as a newcomer will set it in motion again. Special circumstances in themselves make a big difference in the way you will be treated.

We saw in Chapter 8 that Eddy set himself up as an heir apparent in a group with a long history, solidly entrenched in stage III. By trying to change the pecking order, he aroused strong opposition from everyone, because he explicitly threatened their relative positions and statuses in the group. Eddy's aspirations in this environment made his entry stressful.

Another difficult position is succeeding a highly respected, well-liked member, especially a leader. Still suffering the loss of a friend, perhaps almost like a member of a family, such groups ordinarily find it hard to accept the replacement. If the newcomer arrives soon after the predecessor's departure, if no separation procedure helped the group to let go, and if the emotional costs to the group of its loss are little understood, then everyone will have a hard time with the change. In a way, as the new person, we can never take the place of the favorite who came before. Rather, we can and probably should honor that place while making ourselves known and carving out our own niche.

To honor the memory of a person who preceded us, we must *never* disparage his or her accomplishments, which have been shared with those whom you will be working with and they will be proud of them. They will also be more loyal to the person who left than to you, and any undue criticism may brand you an enemy. If as a new manager you are in a position to make changes and wish to do so, invoke the spirit of the respected predecessor. You might suggest that your program *"builds* on the work done before and is probably what he or she would have wanted if he or she had continued." On occasion you can check the changes with the person who left, including suggestions from the ex-employee that may be worthwhile, and thereby receive his or her blessing. The changes you recommend then can bring credit to both of you, preparing your group for transition to your ways of thinking. Acknowledge new accomplishments by the group with "Margaret would have liked that." Use accomplishments of the past as a standard, such as: "The short time it took you under Richard to change the molds on the production line last summer set a new standard for all of us to meet." You can also ask, "How would Paul have done it?" Asking for information *does not* oblige you to do the job in the same way, but it does show that you respect Paul's competence, as well as the group's, and that you want to take full advantage of it. You can continue to invent, so that you are not controlled by the past, and destined to repeat it, by asking, "Now what can we do to improve? Do we have different circumstances now that we must take into consideration?"

This period of honoring your predecessor is also the time to add your own ideas. Alvin Gouldner observed[1] that throughout the world there is a universal norm of reciprocity. By respecting the missing person, you are respecting the other group members, and they are more than likely to treat you respectfully in return. At work, most often, reciprocity can be expected so long as you and the members of your group have similar values and goals. People want to be treated decently and with dignity, and will respond in kind. The extensive efforts to restructure work so that people are given more influence over decisions that affect them, commonly associated with Japanese-style management, are based on this principle. Evidence shows that the method produces the desired results.

The path toward acceptance in a group that has lost a loved member often is perilous, disappointing, and ultimately a failure, leaving behind a trail of hurt feelings. Such was the fate of Jim, Eddy's successor at the bank. Jim was carefully selected as the best from a large number of well-qualified applicants. He approached the job with enthusiasm, ready to pitch in as the new member of the family. He was absolutely unprepared for the constant comparisons between him and Eddy. In response, he tried to imitate Eddy's style, but it didn't fit him. He looked awkward and uncomfortable, heightening the contrast. Eddy was "the standard," and Jim could not live up to it.

Searching for support and acceptance, Jim switched tactics, separating himself from the past and the people who had been close to Eddy. He stopped mentioning him. Others picked up the cue, and Eddy's name thereafter went underground, still mentioned but in more unfavorable comparisons with the newcomer. Eddy, who had been more than willing to help Jim with his transition and provided consultation in the beginning, heard no more from him. Jim cut the tie because he believed that his continuing to listen to Eddy would make it appear to others that Eddy was still in charge. Furthermore, Jim didn't feel he needed Eddy. Confident of his own ability, he felt that he would be recognized and appreciated for them if he were patient and persistent. Time passed with little evidence of improvement, and his frustration intensified. He felt increasingly isolated and paranoid. His paranoia was justified. Members of the group no longer mentioned Eddy openly, but they continued to talk about him among themselves and to meet and speak with him privately. Their attachment to Eddy strengthened rather than weakened, expressed in increased resentment of and resistance to Jim. None of Jim's ideas ever seemed to measure up to Eddy's; Jim couldn't shake Eddy's shadow. It dogged him, limiting his effectiveness and disrupting the group. Eventually, Jim gave up, left in bitterness, feeling that he'd never been given a fair chance to succeed. And he hadn't: he had faced an uphill battle with little understanding or support from the rest of the organization.

On the other hand, Alex, the person who followed Jim, inherited a demoralized group, seeking relief from the disorder that Jim had left behind. The standard to which he was compared was now Jim, who, they reflected, hadn't seemed to do anything right. Often the immediate successor to a beloved employee fails on the job, paving the way for the next person to succeed. Circumstances make a difference. If you follow an ineffective member, as Alex did, you bring relief, become "a savior," and generally have an easier time being accepted. If you replace a much-cared-about and respected person, as Jim did, you are illegitimate, and generally have a harder time. If you expect to upset the traditional hierarchy, as Jim did, you will confront vested interests and face an uphill battle.

You can see how important it is to find out what is really going on in an organization before deciding to join it. Having a reasonably accurate understanding of conditions will help you to plan an entry strategy if you decide to take the job, and it may even persuade you to stay away. Yet the critical information you need about the job and organization is hard to come by. Most people you first meet in the company will put their best foot forward. Tensions and difficulties are often concealed or minimized. You will have to be alert to subtle cues of strained relationships, territorialism, cliques, power centers, and the feelings people have about the person you are replacing. How do you find out what you want to know? Ask questions. Pay attention to the way in which people talk about themselves and others. If you have the opportunity to see people interacting, watch how they treat each other. Some questions to ask are:

- Tell me about the person I am replacing.
- With whom was he or she close?
- What was he or she best known for?
- Did he or she have difficulty with some people?
- Who are they?
- How did they deal with the difficulties?
- Who are the main people I'll be working with?
- What are they best known for?
- What are the luncheon arrangements?
- Who eats with whom?

People who eat together regularly are apt to be close to each other, and therefore to support each other on all kinds of work issues. They also are likely to provide a grapevine, facilitating the flow of information in the organization.

Signs that you will want to notice are hesitations, stuttering, and generalizations such as "We all get along well here," or "He or she is an interesting person," specifics that are explained away, such as "He or she can sometimes be stubborn, but it's not a problem," or joking references to "our fearless leader." What do you do when you pick up these telltale signs? Probe. You can respond with interest by saying "Stubborn? That's interesting. Can you tell me more about it?" Don't, however, push anyone into volunteering more than they seem comfortable doing. After all, you are still a stranger, and insiders will feel disloyal if they seem to be criticizing their colleagues or their organization. Pushed by you to reveal more than they feel they should, they will resent you for it. The information may be useful to you, but avoid setting people against you while you are acquiring it. This is a fine line to walk. You want to know enough about the situation to make intelligent decisions about whether to take the job and how to get started in it, yet you don't want to alienate anybody with your inquiries.

Our suggestion is to let the information accumulate. If you are on the trail of truly unpleasant facts, you are likely to become more and more aware of them in talking with people you meet during recruitment. Be alert and add things up, both positive and negative, as you go along. The picture that develops won't be perfect, but you will be better informed by the time you are ready to make the crucial decision to join up or not, and to plan your entry into the organization.

SPECIAL CASE: ENTRY OF THE CREDENTIALED PROFESSIONAL (DOCTOR, LAWYER, ARCHITECT, ENGINEER, ETC.)

There are, of course, a host of other special circumstances. A common one is a credentialed professional's arrival in a group, such as a medical doctor joining a hospital department, or an electronic engineer coming in to a project team. The credentials are a way of establishing a person's credibility and expertise, without having to try the person out to identify his or her skills. When doctors are hired, they are seen as professionals who have the technical knowledge and skills to start doing the job from day one. Skills are taken as a given and doctors are expected to be able to perform their tasks. Therefore, doctors who join a hospital staff seldom receive much of an orientation beyond the usual introductions and tour of the facilities so that they will know where things are, including their offices. Hospitals do of course have orientation programs, some of them very good, but they are for other employees. Doctors don't attend orientation sessions because it doesn't occur to them that they need them, and they might feel uncomfortable sitting in the company of other employees. Hospitals are still fearsomely hierarchic. Nor do personnel in human-resources departments intrude, because customs (norms) do not accept the questioning of doctors by nonmedical personnel. Finally, the culture of the hospital focuses on the task and responsibility of the individual rather than the group, unless it is specialized, like a trauma team. Therefore, team concepts are not recognized in orienting doctors to their new jobs. They find their own ways to fit in, sometimes with needless and extended discomfort and consequent loss of efficiency. Of course, most doctors do adjust to the changes, but the procedure could be accelerated with planning and attention, using concepts we have discussed here. So far, however, we have seen little inclination in the medical profession to address the nontechnical side of fitting in. Without awareness of a need, no change will come.

SPECIAL CASE: ENTRY INTO A TEMPORARY GROUP, THE PROJECT TEAM

Project teams are common in many organizations, especially in high-technology businesses. They invariably place people in a matrix that has them reporting to more than one boss. Although matrix organizations seem to provide the advantage of spreading scarce resources by allocating them temporarily to tasks that need them, they create a host of problems. For one thing, they violate the age-old rule that requires reporting to only one boss. There is a reason for this rule. It makes organizational life much easier, decision making simpler, cuts confusion for subordinates, puts less strain on communications, doesn't divide loyalties, and demands fewer skills of managers. Matrix organizations are very demanding. The natural tendency of experts assigned to a project is to have less loyalty to it than to their functions (such as electrical engineering). The function is the home base, and its manager often is the sole source of rewards such as promotions, assignments, and salary increases. Under these circumstances, project managers need much skill to generate and maintain commitment to their projects. Understanding the stages in group development will help managers emphasize mechanisms that strengthen ties to the group. Matrices are used in companies like Boeing, IBM, General Dynamics, TRW, but to make project teams effective it takes skill, concentration, consistency, and rewards that reinforce recognition that the individual's contribution to the project team's performance really matters.

A project team is a temporary group. All come to it as newcomers, no matter how long they have been in the company or how often they have been together. As a new group, formed for a specific purpose, it passes predictably through the stages in group development. In these wholly new groups, transitions from stage to stage are most easily noticed. They can be anticipated, and passage through them can be constructively facilitated. Good project managers ease these transitions, whether intuitively or because they have learned to understand and apply group dynamics. Such groups do not, of course, reflect divided loyalty. Members are deeply committed to the project and rely on the merits in their ideas, not formal authority, to influence each other. With all their sophistication in team building, many good project leaders do less well in bringing a newcomer aboard after the project is under way. New members are generally allowed to find their own way, much like the doctor who comes new to a hospital. Awareness that the group will recycle itself after the newcomer's arrival is minimal. Thus, the process is a hit or miss one and usually inefficient.

What can be done to increase awareness and efficiently add a newcomer to a project team? The newcomer, members of the project group, and their manager must first be aware that the group *will* recycle itself. Then the job is facilitating connections, settling the place of the new person in the informal hierarchy, and reassessing and reaffirming norms. In the connecting stage, particular care must be taken to share the project's history, including all relevant technical developments, so that task and personal connections are based on reliable information. Assigning a buddy will undoubtedly help. If as much attention is paid to bringing the new person aboard as to developing the team in the first place, valuable time will be saved, disruption of the group will be minimized, and the value of the new member's fresh perceptions will be maximized.

Because project teams are conspicuous and their worth is obvious, they get a lot of attention in organizations. This popularity offers considerable hope that management of them will continue to improve. Although ad hoc task forces and committees are subject to the laws of group dynamics, training in leading such groups is not given high priority. Thus they suffer from the worst aspects of matrix memberships. No lament in organizations is more common than how poorly meetings are run. It doesn't have to be that way, and applying the concepts in this chapter will help leaders to run meetings better.

SPECIAL CASE: ENTRY OF THE PERMANENT PART-TIMER

Twenty-five percent of the work force consists of permanent part-timers. If large numbers in an organization are part-timers, as in United Parcel Service (UPS), the culture accommodates this phenomenon, but one part-timer in a group may have great difficulty in feeling at home and contributing as much as he or she potentially can to the group's work. Because a part-timer may be absent during rituals such as coffee breaks or lunches, some of the natural vehicles used to make connections aren't available. Nor is as much reinforcement possible through repeated and regular social contact. Out of sight, out of mind describes these people. They can be relegated to permanent second-class status if they get started wrong and nothing is done to change perceptions of them. As the group evolves, their place may become firmly set at the outer margin. Therefore, part-time newcomers need to think doubly hard about how they should conduct themselves when they enter a group of full-timers, and the organization must devise ways of avoiding the almost certain tendency to reduce the part-timer's value to the group. Visibility and contact are the key factors for part-timers. They have to move about, show themselves, write memos, make phone calls, say hello, and chat when appropriate. The organization needs to help by scheduling meetings at times when part-timers can be present; facilitating connections and interaction with a buddy system; remembering to invite them to breaks, parties, lunches, and drinks; and filling them in on work gossip and information that wouldn't otherwise reach them. In other words, permanent employees, managers in particular, should treat part-timers as fully contributing members when they are at work. Managers' behavior is especially crucial because they are the models from whom subordinates get their cues. Such efforts will be noticeably rewarding to all because part-timers are seldom included so thoroughly. In appreciation for being accepted and incorporated as full group members, part-timers will generally respond with superior effort.

SPECIAL CASE: ENTRY OF THE TEMPORARY EMPLOYEE

Temporary help is a rapidly increasing phenomenon in the work place. Because "temps" are not seen as potential members or insiders, they remain perpetual outsiders. Therefore, they are rarely hazed, for hazing is a test for membership and they are not seen as possible candidates, nor are they allowed to join informal groups at work. Out of our sample of twenty-four temps, only one experienced hazing. Although she was classified as temporary, she stayed on the job seventeen months, and her peers began to think of her as permanent. With this shift in perception of her employment status, she was subjected to all the experiences that permanent newcomers go through.

Temporary workers have to be prepared to accept a position outside the social life of the organization. At best they can hope to be treated kindly, even warmly by their colleagues, but real membership will not be available. Permanent workers aren't mean. They don't want to expend the emotional energy to become attached to someone who may soon leave. We have seen how a new member pushes the group to restructure itself, which is also an unsettling experience. As a consequence, permanent employees unconsciously protect themselves by keeping temporary helpers at a distance, a fact of life to which the temporary person must adapt.

SPECIAL CASE: ENTRY AS ADDITIONAL HOURLY WORKER TO UNSKILLED LABOR GROUP

A problem faced in all groups is the tendency to emphasize the task in orienting newcomers to the job, leaving them to figure out for themselves the meaning of the ways in which people relate to each other. Unless a supervisor has the training to treat the group's development as significant, all the effort is likely to be focused on teaching new arrivals how to perform technically. Even this orienting is often perfunctory. Donald F. Roy, a sociologist who studied at first hand hourly work on the shop floor, reported that "introduction to the new job, with its relatively simple machine skills and work routines, was accomplished with what proved to be, in my experience, an all-time minimum of job training. The superintendent and one of the operators gave a few brief demonstrations, accompanied by bits of advice. . . . After a short practice period, at the end of which the superintendent expressed satisfaction with progress and potentialities, I was left to develop my learning curve with no other supervision than that afforded by members of the work group."[2] Though Roy received little help on the technical part of the job, he got no help at all in understanding who was more or less important, what the norms were, or the purpose served by the simpleminded games his fellow workers played on each other every day: "For example, Ike would regularly switch off the power at Sammy's machine whenever Sammy [a fellow employee] made a trip to the lavatory or drinking fountain, and Sammy invariably fell victim to the plot by making an effort to operate [his machine] after returning to the shop. And as the simple pattern went, this blind stumbling into the trap was always followed by indignation and reproach from Sammy, smirking satisfaction from Ike, and mild paternal scolding from George [another employee in the group]." Other repetitive and seemingly mindless behaviors included Ike's daily snatching Sammy's luncheon banana, the sharing of two peaches, and name-calling over whether a window should be left open.

Eventually, Roy realized that the games were rituals that bound the group, increased closeness without open expression of affection (with which the men were uncomfortable), reinforced the pecking order in the group, and relieved boredom. Not until he could recognize their significance and value was Roy able to join the rituals and thus become an accepted group member. This account of machine work in a factory represents experiences at work encountered daily almost everywhere in one form or another. Perhaps you have rituals at work in which you participate but which might seem ridiculous to an outsider, though they are meaningful to you and your fellow workers. In a group observed by one of us, the five members started off every day by asking each other how they were feeling. This opening led to serious exchanges about various ailments, joking about someone's weight, goodnatured ribbing about another's physical condition, and so on. Every morning the same things were said about the same people. Although this behavior looked like a waste of time to the observer, he discovered that it helped hold the group together, being one of the ways in which members showed that they cared about each other.

WHAT TO DO

A newcomer needs to know about the task *and* the social structure of the group he or she is joining. Our surveys show that orientations, whether done formally through programs, or informally, emphasize the task. We have found no instance in which the new arrival is told about the stage of development that the group is in, the ways in which people treat each other, or how a new member is greeted and absorbed into the group. The job of acquiring this important information is left to chance.

SEPARATION RITUALS

We have seen in this chapter how a newcomer is integrated into a work group, and the many special circumstances that make a difference in the way in which a newcomer will be greeted. The feelings group members have for the person who is being replaced often influence the way in which the new member is received into the group. If the person who left was liked very much or even loved, the path for a successor will be very difficult. The transition can, however, be made somewhat easier if group members share their feeling of loss. To cope with a beloved colleague's departure, employees need to understand the mourning process. When you lose someone you care a lot about, you will miss him or her for quite a while. The sense of loss is inevitable, and you can therefore anticipate and prepare for it. First, you should celebrate the departure. Ordinarily, organizations handle this function very well. You have probably joined in farewell parties for those who were leaving; perhaps you have been celebrated in that way. Farewell gatherings are useful ceremonies that allow us to show respect, to express affection, to honor cared-about fellow workers, and to let them know that they may be gone but they won't be forgotten. In most organizations, though, the people who remain behind are expected to adjust rapidly after the party. Because the effect of loss on the work group is often not acknowledged by the manager, an opportunity is missed to get over it in a healthy manner.

The way to cope with mourning is to know what to expect from it. We are indebted to Elisabeth Kübler-Ross, a Swiss psychiatrist, for identifying the stages in adjustment to loss in *On Death and Dying*,[3] based on her work with the terminally ill. Her lessons also apply to the "little deaths" — the departures that we experience in our lives within organizations.

- *Denial* is the first reaction to news of an impending death. The organizational equivalent is news that a highly valued, well-liked fellow worker will soon be leaving. People may refuse to accept the news, believing that it won't really happen, that he or she will have a change of mind, that the organization will find a way to keep the departing one.

- The next stage is *anger*. Facing imminent death, the person feels angry with the doctors or the hospital or even members of the family. In the organization, people are angry with bosses for allowing the colleague to go, or with the person leaving for letting the group down, and with any replacement for daring to take his or her place.

- *Bargaining* follows. For a terminally ill patient, this stage can take the form of promising God to become a better person in exchange for a reprieve. The organization may try to offer more money, a better position, or other inducements to get the person to stay.

- *Depression* grows as the failure of bargaining becomes apparent. In the organization, group members feel listless and glum. The fun seems to have gone out of working together. At this time other members of the group may also decide to leave. The future looks so bleak at the time that they give up and go elsewhere. They may be making a terrible mistake, for depression distorts judgment. But people at such times don't realize that their perceptions are unreliable and thus may make decisions resulting in additional loss, for themselves and for their organization.

- *Acceptance* is the final stage. Reality takes over, putting the leaving in perspective, reminding everyone of the good times but recognizing that the group has the capacity to heal, recover, and continue to perform well. When mourners reach this stage, they can carry on with their lives. They may be sad because they miss the person who has left, but they will not be crippled by the loss.

Organizations can help employees deal more effectively with the departure of well-liked colleagues by taking the next step beyond the party, acknowledging that mourning must take place. People need to find a way to accept their painful feelings and find relief from them. They should be encouraged to talk and understand that the feelings associated with denial, anger, bargaining, depression, and acceptance are natural, inevitable, and healthy. When the feelings are expressed, they assume true proportions, feelings are less distorted, and judgment is more reliable. When feelings are suppressed, people will act them out, often in unhealthy ways such as quitting or sabotaging a replacement. The manager can actively help a group get through the mourning stage by allowing and even encouraging talk about the member who has left. A newcomer can be patient and understanding, taking no offense at the others' reactions to him or her that are stimulated by a predecessor's departure. People who are left behind can give themselves time to "get over it," knowing that doing so will take time and patience. If managers, newcomers, and group members give themselves time, are not afraid to talk, and share their feelings about the loss, they will be well rewarded. Reality will gradually replace the distorted perceptions that are aroused by strong feelings associated with loss, and the group can then go on to develop effectively.

We do not propose that the loss of a well-loved member in a close group is equal to the feelings about the death of a friend or family member, but we do believe that we are dealing with similar mourning phenomena; that is, living with an empty chair, whether at the family dinner table or behind a desk. The stages in mourning are essentially the same, though felt much less strongly in an organization than in a family. Therefore they should be recognized as important and not treated lightly.

MANAGING IS

Leading
Coaching
Training
Helping
Inspiring
Challenging
Supporting
Encouraging

But most of all,
Caring.

The Manager's Opportunity

FOR new executives, the first days, weeks, months on a job are the most treacherous period in their employment. Allerton-Heinze Associates, an executive recruiting firm in Chicago, states that turnover for executives is higher during the first two years in a new job than at any other time. They attribute the high turnover to the failure of organizations to effectively manage the incoming executive's integration into the organization. It is our experience that persons at all levels in an organization — professionals, hourly employees, as well as executives — are at greater risk during their entry period on a new job than at most other times in their working lives. This book is devoted to improving the transit through this passage. The benefits in better managing the assimilation of newcomers are clear. They will be happier and more productive; organizational costs will be lower, and permanent work groups will suffer less disruption. Our focus in this chapter is on the hiring manager's responsibility for managing the entry process of newcomers more effectively.

THE IMPORTANCE OF THE EMPLOYMENT INTERVIEW

We have referred to the importance of the first impressions that newcomers make on the people with and for whom they will work. The impressions managers make on the newcomer also matter greatly; the first opportunity that the hiring manager has to favorably influence his or her prospective employees is when they meet in the employment interview. Both interviewer and candidate want information that will influence their decisions — to hire or not and to accept the job or not. Information isn't confined to facts that are exchanged, such as the organization's compensation, benefits, hours, products, and mission and the candidate's qualifications, experience, and aspirations. It also includes impressions formed about personality fit and how the organization feels about its employees. For the candidate, the interview is the first indication of how he or she is likely to be treated in the organization. The interview is a two-way street, with each of the parties developing critical impressions of the other.

In order for the manager and candidate to get all the information they need, and to set the stage for the new employee's rapid, constructive, productive integration into the organization, the manager must create and maintain a good climate in the interview.

CREATING A GOOD INTERVIEW CLIMATE

A good interview climate starts with the setting, which can convey imaginativeness, seriousness, busyness, or frugality, but it should be consistent with some attitudes about work that you would like to reinforce in the candidate. The interview room should be protected against interruptions and distracting noises. Above all, make it possible for candidates to feel that they are the center of attention for the time that you are together. Have two comfortable chairs, either across a desk if you prefer formality, or facing each other with nothing between the two of you if you wish to be more informal. How far apart you stay will depend on the comfort the two of you need. At first, you may be farther apart, representing your lack of knowledge of each other. As the interview progresses, you can try edging closer to the employment candidate, suggesting your increasing comfort with each other. If the interviewee leans back or retreats in response to your approach, you know that you are going beyond the distance that he or she feels comfortable with. If you furnish ashtrays, a signal about your attitude toward smoking on the job, these should be empty. The sun should not shine into the candidate's eyes, and telephone interruptions should not be permitted. Don't hurry the interview even if you are pressed for time. Have a written list of questions to ask uniformly of all candidates so that you know what facets you're comparing and can think about how and when you will ask them. Be prepared, too, with the information you will want to furnish about the job, the company, its products or services, its vision, workers, benefits, advantages, problems, and work climate.

The kinds of questions that produce the best answers are those which have a follow-up, such as: "Tell me more about . . . ," or "Explain this further," or "What did you mean by . . . ?" or "How did you feel about . . . ?" These are all open-ended questions, as opposed to the more difficult closed questions, which can be answered by a yes or a no, but which make you do all the work because you must be prepared with the next question.

Your body posture must communicate attentiveness. Look the candidate in the eye while you talk; don't doodle, tap your pencil on the desk, wiggle your foot, or show other signs of boredom. Candidates are obviously anxious during interviews, and reassuring words are always helpful in relaxing them. Try saying, "That's interesting," or "I'm glad you mentioned that," or "That's good," or "Aha," as opposed to "Mmm," or even worse — silence. Unless you have a specific reason for putting a candidate under stress, you are likely to conduct a better interview with more relaxed conditions. If you see that the candidate is very nervous, you may even mention it by saying interviews are difficult for a lot of people, that most people are tense during them, and that it's perfectly normal to feel that way. You might offer the candidate a glass of water or a hot drink.

If you're interviewing for higher-level jobs, it is appropriate to interact in a collegial manner, asking opinions about relevant matters. Remember that anyone you are interviewing may one day be your boss. If you are interviewing a woman who raised a family before returning to work, ask her to think of things she has done representing skills that might be applicable to the job. If you are interviewing candidates from different cultures and for whom English is a second language, be aware that the language barrier puts them at a disadvantage because it increases tension, often making it more difficult for them to articulate their thoughts. You must do the best you can to learn about the candidate by being patient and willing to listen carefully. When you don't understand, ask to have the statement repeated. If the language barrier is severe, you may arrange for the person to return with a translator. Your attentiveness, your caring, your warmth, and your patience will make an important first impression on the candidate. An interviewer who works in a large bank described how much first impressions on candidates count. She always managed to leave them with such good feelings about the bank that, even though they were not hired, many of them opened accounts and became customers.

After the interview, you will want to reflect on what you have learned about the prospective employee before making a decision on hiring. You will also want to fix impressions in your mind for future use if the person joins you. For these reasons, and to keep your conclusions as objective as possible, make notes both during the interview and immediately after the candidate leaves. Otherwise, you will be surprised at how much you will forget, and you will be unaware of how much you can distort, particularly if you have interviewed more than one candidate that day.

A point about interviewing that is often missed is its healthy effect on the interviewer. Studies show that alert interviewers become aware of features in their organization that they had long taken for granted. A candidate's comments, such as: "You have a nice view from this window," or "People dress more conservatively here than in other places I have worked," may provide you with new insights about your organization. They may also provide information about work preferences of employees in general, of technical developments in your industry, or characteristics of the competition that can eventually lead to new policy decisions. It has also been suggested that interviewers who say positive things about the organization feel reinforced in those feelings, increasing their attachment to it.[1]

Thus, the manager's interview with a prospective employee, which is sometimes seen as a burdensome task to be performed as quickly as possible, is an extraordinarily rich opportunity to develop oneself as well as get needed information and get a new person off to the right start.

THE FIRST DAY FROM THE MANAGER'S PERSPECTIVE

Spending a little time anticipating the new employee's first day at work can bring a very large payoff. Managers should be prepared to discuss these four features of the job: *the setting* (where), *the people* (who), *the task* (what), and *the norms* (how).

The *setting* is both the work place itself and the rest of the premises. The *people* are those who are related in some way to the work of the new employee. The *task* is what the newcomer is responsible for and how it relates to the whole organization's output. The *norms* deal with the unwritten rules that govern the behaviors of the people at work.

The scenario for a first day at work could be as follows. The employee comes in to the supervisor's office for an initial meeting about that first day. The manager has a checklist of items to be covered, such as a tour of the premises, an introduction to people and to things to do, a review of the job, a few words about the culture of the organization, paperwork with which the new person should be familiar, and training materials. If a buddy is assigned for guidance, he or she should be alerted, and, at an appropriate time, introduced to the newcomer.

This sample checklist of items to be covered on a new employee's first day may be helpful in designing one of your own if your company does not have one:

- Employee's duties and work standards
- Probationary period
- Performance evaluations: frequency and standards
- Attendance and work hours
- Annual leave, vacation policies
- Overtime (if applicable)
- Lunch periods and breaks
- Time cards (if applicable)
- Restrooms
- Supplies and equipment
- Parking and transportation
- How to notify if late or sick
- Responsibilities and organization of department
- Applicable department regulations
- Safety practices
- Department EEO policy[2]

This list will not fit every manager's purposes, but it illustrates the kinds of things you may want to cover. Not only is it important to go through the list and ask if there are any questions, it is desirable to have new employees sign a copy of the checklist indicating that they have indeed had an opportunity to discuss each item. Signing the list also reinforces for the manager the importance of covering each item on the list.

A first day at work is always stressful, and the new employee will forget much of what you say. Therefore, the material needs to be reviewed at a later date. Your preparations will demonstrate care to the new employee. Pay attention to the questions that seem to trouble the employee and ask: "How do you feel?" "Did you have problems finding the place?" "Are you a bit apprehensive?" It is normal to feel apprehensive on one's first day, and helping the new employee to talk about the feeling can lessen his or her anxiety by making it acceptable.

THE SETTING

The first thing the manager should do is give the new employee a tour of the work place, pointing out the washroom facilities, the coffee machine, the cafeteria, where to go on breaks, and whatever else one needs to know about the space. Formal orientation programs often take newcomers on a tour of the premises, which builds identity with the company, whether it is in a large building, several stories high or simply a couple of offices. New employees sense a manager's reaction to the surroundings. A feeling of pride will be noticed by the new employee, who is then likely to start feeling that way, too.

THE PEOPLE

The next step is to introduce the employee to the people with whom he or she will be working. We suggest distributing a memo to announce the arrival of the employee, calling a meeting for introductions to the work group, and then going around to meet the new colleagues one by one.

The written announcement prepares people for the newcomer. It creates anticipation and conveys the feeling that the newcomer is valued by the organization and management. The advance notice also takes away some of the mystery that may surround a new worker, inviting less speculation. The meeting with the group provides everyone with a simultaneous first exposure, reducing the potential for prejudice or distortion conveyed through the grapevine by those who meet the newcomer first. The group meeting is also an opportunity for the new employee to make a statement, ask and respond to questions, and thereby influence the first impressions of others. The personal introduction to colleagues, one by one, is evidence of the manager's support for the newcomer, and a chance to get each individual relationship started differently as appropriate. The manager might emphasize things the newcomer and an insider have in common, or areas for them to explore that might be mutually helpful. Here is a chance to get information across that is uniquely useful to two individuals rather than to the whole group.

We have noticed that some managers leave new employees wholly on their own — even to managing their own introductions. The weakness of such neglect should seem obvious. Most newcomers are likely to manage themselves poorly, thrown into this circumstance. Other managers use only a memo, group meeting, or personal introduction. Although putting less effort into a new employee's introduction saves time, it is a savings dearly bought. In the long run, the cost is likely to exceed the short-run benefits of such savings.

The Buddy System

One of the best ways to smooth introduction of a newcomer is to assign a fellow employee to answer the new worker's questions. What is obvious to an oldtimer will be totally confusing to a newcomer. Often newcomers are unwilling to ask questions for fear of sounding stupid. A recent study shows that white women and Asians have more trouble asking questions and getting information about their jobs than do white men, Hispanics, or blacks. Women didn't want to ask questions because they were afraid to be seen as stupid; Asians, because they didn't want their bosses to lose face by having to explain something or repeat it, a sign the boss didn't do it right the first time.[3]

The person in charge of the new employee's introduction should be assigned to the task beforehand and be given information on the person's background and qualifications. Selecting a buddy is an important decision, because that person must have enough credibility with the rest of the work group to help the new protégé gain acceptance by proxy, yet not be ranked so high above the newcomer as to be intimidating. We call this person a "buddy" to differentiate the term from "mentor" and "sponsor," which suggest long-term involvement with the protégé's career. The buddy system is a temporary arrangement to help the newcomer get on board and be accepted by the others. The buddy spends time with the newcomer, answering questions, introducing coworkers, including him or her in the informal groupings that occur spontaneously, and inviting the newcomer to join in the planned events.

The buddy must be both *willing* and *able* to perform this function. In a number of companies, being a buddy is seen as a privilege, and people compete for the opportunity. In others, being a buddy is perceived as a burden, and people feel that it demands too much of their time. An unwilling buddy is not going to be very effective, for a lot of patience is needed to answer questions that may seem self-evident. Some sort of organizational reward, such as an increase in pay, a special bonus, praise during a performance review, or even public recognition for helping newcomers, should be established to stimulate oldtimers to assist newcomers. Allowances must be made because buddies who spend time with newcomers may not get all their work done on time.

Surprisingly, some companies have assigned employees who are marginally acceptable performers to teach newcomers with the hope that by having to explain and demonstrate the necessary skills again, the marginal employee's commitment to do better will be reinforced. These companies have found that this approach improves the performance of the teacher as well as the pupil. The arrangement can also work in reverse, though, because the newcomer can learn bad work habits from the marginal employee. But the plan is worth considering.[4]

Introducing Coworkers

The new employee should be introduced to all the people with whom he or she will work. We recommend giving him or her a list of the people, their functions, and their locations. The manager should ask each person whose work will be related to the new person's job to set aside time for chatting during the day, so that the first day's agenda is filled with people to talk to. Of course, sometimes this attention will be neither necessary nor feasible, and the new employee need only meet briefly with the immediate superior and the people on whom he or she will be immediately dependent.

For higher-level jobs, a structured approach to the integration of a new manager into the organization is called the transition meeting.[5] Although characteristics of the plans may vary, it generally includes four parties: the departing manager, the incoming manager, the manager's immediate staff, and a trained facilitator. Each plays a role in a meeting designed to bring the new manager constructively into the organization. The transition meeting's objectives are as follows:

- "To encourage people to express what they were committed to.
- To get to know them.
- To learn what the group was trying to do and why.
- To discover their fears with regard to interruption of their progress.
- To gain their confidence so that he could work with them without threatening their mode of operation."

Such objectives reflect a new manager's desire to maintain the productive and successful ways in which the group was working. In other instances, the objectives might be different, reflecting issues appropriate to those situations. In Chapter 11 we describe successful use of a transition type meeting by the General Electric Company, which is called "The New Manager Assimilation Process."

THE TASK

What to do on that first day will vary depending on the level at which the person has been hired. At the lower levels, new workers should be given a task. This assignment can be reading materials, observing a person at work, or participating in a training program — anything that fulfills the learning needs of the new employees and gets them going.

At all levels, a new employee needs to know where papers are filed, what service is to be provided, what products are to be made, and what things need to be checked. Generally, newcomers should be given a description appropriate to the job, detailing all that needs to be done to meet the job requirements. To perform well, people need to know what is expected of them. Also explain what resources are available, such as information, equipment, and people.

THE NORMS

Norms prescribe *how* people behave in the work group and *how* jobs get done. Each organization has its own unwritten rules to which its members adhere. The new person's manager should meet in advance with the members of the group, or at least its leader, to inform them of the newcomer's responsibilities, expertise if any, and other background that might be useful for the members to know in order to integrate the newcomer into the group's activities. Again, one person should be responsible for informing the new worker about the group's tasks, its preferred ways of working, its norms. These may include:

We take turns in talking //
We're always interrupting one another

We kid around a lot //
We get down to work right away

We take breaks only at prescribed times //
We come and go as we please

We disagree a lot and get into really heated arguments //
We're careful with each other, trying not to ruffle too many
   feathers

We defer to a leader (or an expert) //
We don't have a leader; everyone's the same

We're a very tightly knit group; it will be hard for you to break
   in //
We're a very loose group, and you'll have no trouble entering

These are some of the norms governing groups. Many norms are not obvious and therefore are difficult to explain to someone outside the group. It is incumbent on the new member to observe coworkers' behavior and figure out the norms; it is the manager's responsibility to point them out.

Some norms are functional, some are dysfunctional. Some norms may be functional for a group, but dysfunctional for the company. Let us say the company has a regulation about not smoking, but the members of one unit disregard the regulation; their norm is to break the rule. For the people who like to smoke, this attitude would work very well. A fire hazard, though, may have been ignored. To find out whether a norm is functional or dysfunctional, a manager can do a *norms census*, getting together with the people who work for him or her and listing norms that they work under. If the staff is large, it can be split into groups of six to eight people. Each group works in the same way, coming up with a list of norms, which is then publicly displayed and discussed in order to decide if they are functional or dysfunctional. The lists from the different groups can then be combined to create a set of norms for the entire unit. The value of small groups is that they give everyone a chance to speak up. We have found little difference in the output of these small groups because norms are widely known. The next step is to take the norms that don't seem to work well and see what can be done about eliminating them or reducing their negative impact.

This information about functional and dysfunctional norms, which is usually not available to newcomers for many months, should be communicated early on to facilitate integration. Doing a norms census will first identify the norms, then make it possible to tell a newcomer about them. Without a norms census, a manager may overlook some of the more important ones, especially because they can so easily be taken for granted by those living with them. Pointing out norms to newcomers will save them much time and pain otherwise wasted in figuring them out, and will save everyone aggravation caused by norms not followed out of ignorance.

Although taking a norms census from time to time is very useful for a manager and the work group, it does require that employees be open in front of the boss. Without the high level of trust that is necessary for such candid sharing, a norms census may actually be misleading. Some managers may even be unwilling to engage in a procedure that cannot be relied on to produce a realistic picture of what is going on. If the mutual trust is missing, the manager is better advised to rely on buddies to introduce newcomers to the ways in which things are done in the organization.

If a manager wants to build trust that seems to be missing in the work group, he or she will probably be better served by consultants to help develop trust, than by trying to produce it himself or herself. Consultants, who are perceived as objective and not allied with the manager or with the employees, are almost indispensable in diminishing defensiveness and resolving conflicts that inevitably arise when practices are revealed that may be embarrassing for manager or employees or both.

WHAT CAN AND SHOULD MANAGERS DO ABOUT HAZING?

Although hazing is a norm, we treat it as a special case because more often than not it is misunderstood. Hazing evidently is here to stay. As long as we have human groups, we will have membership issues and rites of passage from being an outsider to becoming a member. If hazing is mild and does not slow integration of new employees, then leave well enough alone. When it creates stress in individuals, causes delays in learning the new job by hindering training, or creates exclusion from the work groups, then the organization pays a price. The high turnover rate, absenteeism, tardiness, and low job commitment caused by hazing are beyond estimating. An unhappy worker is an ineffective worker. Few employees can be high producers in an atmosphere that leaves them feeling alienated. When individuals and the organization are victimized by hazing, when its consequences are negative, then supervisors must work to stop it. And because the new employee may be afraid to report the practice, it is the manager's job to be aware of it. When the hazing is harmless, the manager must explain to the newcomer that it is normal and usual, that the new person is not being singled out, and that surviving the ordeal is a question of time and demonstrating the ability to take it graciously. Being forewarned will make the hazing bearable, perhaps even fun. When the hazing is severe enough to cause dysfunction in the work place, the manager must intervene and help the hazers find other means for testing the newcomer, if that is what is going on, or reduce the teasing by pointing out the price being paid in slowing integration.

Hazing is different from harassment and the criteria should remain clear: hazing is something all newcomers go through, and is meant to incorporate them into the group. Harassment is done to selected people to keep them out or make them quit. All managers should be alert to hazing so that it will become a function which they monitor and control, instead of a repetition of old rituals which they allow or sanction, and which has become dysfunctional for today's circumstances.

The Culture

One of the more significant events on an employee's first day is the initial meeting with the immediate supervisor to discuss not only what the person will be doing, but also the company's culture. We mean by culture what the company is all about, whether it is to make the best product, to make it in the cheapest way, to render broad service to as large a population as possible, or to give in-depth service to a few.

One of our children, a very fine carpenter and cabinetmaker, got a summer job with a construction company that needed to have work done as quickly and cheaply as possible. He was appalled at the shoddiness of the company's product, and the company was upset with his perfectionism at the price of slowness. Obviously, employee and company were not a good fit. Speed and quality don't always go together, and it helps to know where the major focus is to be. The norm of this construction company was to get houses up as fast as it could; attention to detail and good workmanship were not important. The value system was acceptance of imperfection and the culture focus was low cost. Had this message been spelled out by the supervisor when our son was hired, he, his boss, and his organization might have resolved their differences without the frustration all experienced later.

Organizational culture can be summed up in one sentence: "This is the way we do things around here, and this is what you can expect." Although the setting, the people, the task, the norms, and the culture should all be discussed by the manager on the first day, it is not the end of the the manager's responsibility to integrate the new-comer into the organization. Integration is an ongoing process which should continue until the new employee masters the job and is accepted. The fitting in may take months, depending on the complexity of the job, the number of coworkers employed, and the job's importance. Ultimately, of course, it is desirable that new employees have the skill to help themselves get on board effectively. One of the better ways is to learn the skill of observing others' behavior. The ability to observe, to make mental notes of what seems significant, and to remember to use the information when relevant is valuable to everyone. This ability becomes even more critical in a new job situation.

AFTER THE FIRST DAY

The help that the manager gives to the new employee on the first day is only the first step in a progression that will bring him or her up to speed. It should continue for as long after the first day as necessary. For some people in some jobs, especially if a buddy system is used, checking in occasionally over the next few weeks will be sufficient. For other jobs and other employees, closer contact will be needed longer. The time devoted to this orientation period should be well rewarded, producing desirable attitudes that persist and help shape the character of the new employee and, ultimately, of the entire organization.

TRIBAL PRACTICES[1]

In some tribes
they scar their faces;
we put paint on ours

In some tribes
they pierce noses;
in ours it's earlobes

In some tribes
they beat drums;
in ours, we pray and sing

In some tribes
ritual foods are eaten;
we sprinkle holy water

In some tribes
the priests wear feathers;
ours wear jeweled robes

Baptisms or circumcisions,
communions or bar mitzvahs,
weddings or funerals,
tribal rites all
with jubilation or meditation
in trances or with hymns

The ancients' prescriptions,
our sacred obligations,
our rites of passage,
our badges of belonging
to a specific tribe

A member of,
a part of,
recognized as,
remembered as,
having something in common
with others like us.

Company Policy:
Formal Orientation Programs

IT'S Joan's first day with the XYZ Company (the company's real name and those of individuals are disguised), known as the community's most desirable employer. She's excited to be there and a little anxious. Although she feels special because she was picked from a field of candidates, she is still uneasy about starting work. She worries whether she will meet expectations and if the job will be as challenging as it appears. She wonders if she will like her coworkers and if they will like her. She hopes that she made the right choice; after all, she did have other attractive opportunities.

Before she actually reports to her new boss, she is scheduled to participate in an all-day orientation program. She is told she is lucky because it is held only when enough people have been hired to make it worthwhile; some people waited weeks before they went. The human-resources director is proud of the program, which he designed to reinforce favorable feelings about the company, to make newly hired employees feel at home, and to help them work into their jobs sooner.

Joan arrived fifteen minutes early for the orientation session. Three or four others had already arrived, and were looking awkward and saying nothing to one another. The room was set up like an auditorium, with about forty seats; it had no windows, and the walls were lined with tweed drapes whose supports had broken away from the wall, leaving the fabric hanging loosely. The light was adequate, but the room wasn't bright. "Not cheery," Joan thought, and it certainly didn't lift her spirits. A podium, microphone, and table were lined up in front of the chairs. The room soon began to fill. Joan talked to people as they entered, quietly introducing herself, but soon ran out of things to say, noticing uneasily that almost everyone else was more casually dressed than she. Feeling out of place, she sat down to look and feel less conspicuous.

The program started on time as Tom introduced himself as director of human resources and host for the day. He welcomed everyone and outlined the agenda. Lunch would be from 12:00 to 1:00 in the company cafeteria. Joan was glad she hadn't brown-bagged it after all, although she hadn't been sure whether she should. As Tom spoke about XYZ and its value system, Joan brightened. This information was what she had hoped to hear, and she looked forward to the speakers who would follow. On the schedule for the day was a slide and tape presentation about the company's history and organization, and talks by the manager of operations on the product line, the head of security on plant security, an executive officer on ethics, the benefits supervisor on benefits, and a maintenance supervisor on plant safety.

In a midmorning fifteen-minute break, everyone stretched. It now seemed easier for people to talk with each other, and Joan struck up a conversation with Adrienne, who was sitting next to her. It turned out to be a fortunate meeting because Adrienne was a fellow programmer who'd already been with the company for two weeks. With something in common, Joan felt she'd found a friend. She didn't even go to the vending machine in the corridor for a drink, glad instead to enjoy the connection. It made her feel less strange, alone, and anxious. The break ended and the morning moved on. The information was important, and Joan tried to stay alert, but after three straight hours of lectures, she found her attention wandering. Even Tom looked bored, although he brightened each time he prepared to introduce a speaker. Joan was distracted by his apparent lack of interest.

Lunch was an occasion to sit with others if you pushed yourself in, four to six to a table. People introduced themselves, and "old-timers" with one to four weeks on the job told what it was like for them at XYZ. The conversation became more animated. It all sounded pretty good to Joan, and she wished she had more time to mix with still more of the people who were there. "At least," she thought, "I got to know a few of them, especially Adrienne, in my department."

The afternoon session picked up where the morning left off. More lectures, information, and finally an opportunity to ask questions when the benefits were explained. Another break came and went, but this time Joan lined up at the vending machine for a drink. Soon the program was over, and Tom sent everyone on their way with wishes for a great future with the company.

Joan was glad she had attended the program at the beginning of her employment, even though her head was swimming with information. It was far more than she could handle at one time, and she realized she'd have to check to see exactly what she should do to sign up for each of the benefits. It was also unsettling to have so much emphasis placed on being like a close family, and on meeting the needs of customers as individuals, because during the day in that stuffy, ill-lit, shabbily decorated room she felt that she had been treated impersonally. "If only everyone had had name tags, it would have been easier to make contact. Why must all classrooms and conference halls have chairs in rows?" At lunch when they had sat at round tables, they could see each other and everyone could join in. She was sure that helped people to get to know each other more easily. In fact, it was Adrienne and her luncheon partners whom she remembered best, liked most, and felt closest to. They had been able to talk to each other, and the next time they met, she knew that they'd feel good about it.

GUIDELINES FOR EFFECTIVE ORIENTATION PROGRAMS

We believe that Joan's experience is typical. Our interviews with people who have gone through orientation programs suggest that what happened to Joan is the rule rather than the exception. It wasn't bad, mind you; there was a lot of good in it. Joan and her colleagues reported on an evaluation form that the orientation was valuable. But given its purpose, and the effort put into it, it wasn't good enough; more could have been accomplished.

After listening to our reactions to their orientation program, XYZ improved it by observing these directions:

- Give dress instructions for the orientation program — that is, business or casual clothes. Give an example of appropriate dress.

- Provide information about eating arrangements, such as availability of cafeteria food and what others are likely to do — brown-bag it or buy food.

- Choose a room that is cheerful, bright, and appealing, showing that you care about the people who'll be in there. It is now well known that surroundings, including space, color, and acoustics, affect mood. The environment can reinforce the message you are sending or contradict it. Every setting, no matter how humble, can reflect some of the values you are trying to convey. Neglecting such simple and elementary considerations is inexcusable.

- Have name tags ready in large, readable type, identifying title and department (Tester, Quality Assurance, Building E) in the organization.

- Have soft drinks (including decaffeinated and diet drinks) and breakfast rolls for early arrivals. The food-and-drink table provides a spot around which people can gather. It also gives a natural, not contrived opportunity to talk to each other. As soon as a person makes a connection with at least one other, he or she will feel more at home, less strange, and more a part of the organization. That connection encourages other attachments and loyalties by increasing the person's receptiveness to them. It should be clear by now that facilitating personal connections must be one of the major objectives in every orientation program. Connections are valuable in their own right, but also lead to many other constructive relationships that can bear directly on how well work is later performed.

- At the morning and afternoon breaks, have soft drinks and food ready in the meeting room. By break time, everyone will feel less shy, simply because they've been in a room together all morning. If efforts have been made to help people meet each other, they will seize the opportunity around a food table to get to know one another even better. Urge people to mingle and introduce themselves. They need this permission, encouragement, and legitimization; such an important part of the orientation program should not be left to accident.

- Seat people at round tables, six to eight at a table. After the host's introduction and outline of the agenda, which should also be distributed in writing, have people at each table introduce themselves to one another. Place cards should be on each table so that no one has to test their ability to memorize names. Some companies ask people to tell something about themselves that is different, unusual, or funny. The humor breaks the tension, makes each person feel special, and gives everyone something to talk about together. Other companies feel that such sharing is an invasion of privacy and prefer to stick to name, job, and location. Make your choice consistent with the values of your organization. Whatever you do, try to avoid auditorium seating arrangements. Studies of classroom behavior show that the seating arrangement can influence the number of relationships formed, and their durability.

- At appropriate intervals, ask people to discuss what they have heard and prepare two questions they want answered. Have each group ask their questions before the whole group. The discussion at each table will reinforce the presentation, raise meaningful questions that couldn't be answered in the discussion, predispose everyone to listen to the questions as they're asked, and consequently, the answers to them. Engaging people in this way is energizing. Six hours of presentations is hard to listen to. We've been in programs during which the host has the audience stretch every couple of hours just to get the blood flowing and brain oxygenated. If the host believes in stretching, asking people to do so won't seem awkward. The audience will respond happily and the energy level afterward will be noticeably higher.

- At the end of the day, give people at each table a moment to say goodbye to each other. When they see each other again, during work, meeting will be easier because openers won't be necessary; these people already have a connection.

- Rotate scheduled hosts and presenters so that they don't get bored. Joan noticed that Tom acted uninterested when he wasn't on. In fact, the program had become so routine that he no longer noticed the slippage in his own freshness or others' attention. His perceptions were dulled by routine and therefore unreliable. Without information from other sources, the program was doomed to stagnation. Also, interaction in the program will keep presenters alert and interested and the audience attentive.

A Basic Orientation Program

Orientation has three aspects: information provided before the person goes to work, information provided at work, and training to do the job. Guidelines for each follow:

1. **Providing Information Before Work Begins**
   - Be brief — but use at least one day
   - Cover:
     a) Company history
     b) Company values
     c) Company organization
     d) Company products and services
     e) Benefits (compensation may need particular time and attention)
     f) Safety
     g) Security
     h) Site and facilities
   - Make sure that the procedures reinforce the messages about values that are given and describe realistically experiences the employee will have.
   - Have the employee participate by involving him/her in some discussion of the subject.
   - Observe the guidelines for facilitation described in the XYZ case.
   - Arrange for everyone to receive the information listed above before starting work, even if in abbreviated form. Many companies conduct information briefings on a given day

once a week, once a month, or when they have enough new employees to justify one. Employees hired between briefings then wait three days, three weeks, sometimes many months to officially get basic information about their work and the organization. Employees we have interviewed who endured these long waits have resented them and felt they had missed something vital; the loss is unnecessary. Organizations should develop a short introductory message to give new employees who won't be scheduled for a regular briefing until later.

2. **Providing Information at Work**
   - Arrange for introductions:
     a) within the work unit
     b) with others outside the work unit with whom the new person will have to interact
   - Explain:
     a) Norms
     b) Rules
     c) Practices
   - Show:
     a) Work place
     b) Critical work areas
     c) Facilities
   - Start new employees with clearly assigned, meaningful tasks.
   - Assign responsibilities for introducing the newcomer to the work place, to the supervisor or buddy, or even to subordinates as a group.
   - Use a checklist to be sure everything is done that is supposed to be done. Have it signed by the new employee and the supervisor.
   - Forward the signed checklist to the personnel or human-resources office for filing.

3. **Providing Training**
   - Providing job knowledge and developing skills can be accomplished by any combination of:

a) On-the-job instruction by supervisor, buddy, peers, trainers
b) Outside courses
c) Inside courses

A significant aspect of orientation that is infrequently done in formal orientation programs is the integration of new employees and their families into the social fabric of the community. Values in our society are changing rapidly. Both spouses increasingly share responsibility for deciding where the family will live. With more women working, we have more two-income families to consider. The working as well as social needs of both spouses need to be taken into consideration during orientation.

Some Innovative Orientation Programs

J. M. SMUCKER CORPORATION

At J. M. Smucker, a food processor employing 1,400 people, with 500 in its headquarters in Orrville, Ohio, orientation begins with interviewing of applicants. After passing through the initial screening in the human resources department, everyone goes through a series of interviews, from six to twelve for managers at least up to the officer level, and up to five interviews for nonsupervisors. The chain interviews increase the likelihood of a good match between the requirements of the job and the new employee. They also protect against letting one impression, good or bad, drive the hiring decision, and they give applicants an early feel for the company, its operations, and the people who work for it. Chain interviews permit initial bonding with many people across a lot of organizational boundaries.

Orientation is well under way before the employee reports for work. Then the hiring manager takes over. He or she is personally responsible for on-the-job training and additional structured orientation covering four sessions, one a week, supported by professionally produced slide and tape presentations on the company's history, product lines, benefits, and management system. Each meeting includes discussion of the material covered by the visual aids. Thus Smucker invests in a lot of high-quality time to be sure that the right person is chosen for the job, feels welcome, begins to form meaningful work relationships early, and personally learns the ropes from the manager. Notice that the slide and tape material is a constant, including both facts about products and benefits, and basic company values embedded in history and the management system. The proceedings that the applicant participates in reinforce the strong message that people and their development do matter at Smucker's.

HARRAH'S

Harrah's, a well-known and highly regarded hotel and casino chain, owned by the Holiday Corporation, spells out the steps in its integration program in great detail. It has three aspects: orientation before working, assignment to a sponsor on the first day of work, and task training.

Phase 1: New-Employee Orientation: All employees, front line through management with few exceptions, attend the New Hire Orientation (NHO) before starting on their jobs. The objective is to motivate employees to high performance and reduce turnover. Turnover in the casino industry is high and costly. In 1979, the year before Harrah's New Hire Orientation program was introduced, the company's turnover of regular full-time employees was 83.4 percent on an employee base of 3,401. By 1985, it had dropped to 40 percent. A conservative estimate of savings from reduced turnover for the six years the program has been in effect is more than $3 million. Also, productivity has improved, learning time has decreased, and customer service is better. Since more people return to Harrah's as a consequence, revenues have also risen. A major goal for all Harrah's employees is to deliver service of such high quality that customers will want to come back. Therefore, Harrah's not only wants to keep good, high-performing employees on the job, it wants them to feel good about being there. The belief is that satisfied employees produce satisfied customers.

Harrah's orientation for new employees not only gives them the substantive knowledge and skills they need to succeed, it treats them as the company wants their customers treated — individually, courteously, with dignity and respect. Look at the way in which the

New Hire Orientation lives up to this theme. For the twenty to thirty
new employees who go through it at a time, this is how it starts:

1. The training coordinator greets all new hires at the front door.
2. The training coordinator checks new hires in, gives them their
   identification name tags.
3. An office clerk takes new hires, in groups of four to six, to a
   coffee area to take pictures of them and point out where refresh-
   ments are.
4. After the check-in is completed, the training coordinator takes
   the new hires to the orientation room.

The newcomers learn a number of things in this brief welcome to
the orientation program. From the personal attention received from
the training staff, they find out that they are in fact important. They
realize that this sense of personal value is conveyed by being treated
individually, with courtesy, dignity, and respect. They learn that the
customer can be made to feel the same way by similar treatment.
Later in the orientation program and at work, the importance of
treating employees and customers with courtesy, dignity, and respect at all times is consistently reinforced. Immediately after people
are seated in the orientation room, the program starts. In the first
session, the new employees are introduced to the staff, then welcomed and congratulated on their employment and given information on facilities for personal needs (restrooms, water fountains,
vending machines, rest periods, lunch) and the day's agenda.

An officer of the company then addresses the group and reinforces the New Hires program's selectiveness by citing figures on the
low percentage of applicants who pass the screening. He or she
stresses the company's values (service, courtesy, respect) for customers and employees alike, and shows how Harrah's is the industry leader. As you can see, pride is emphasized, in Harrah's and in
oneself.

The pace now changes, as everyone participates in a problem-
solving exercise in groups of five or six, to illustrate some of the
principles that guide Harrah's Quality of Work Life and Participative
Management efforts. New workers experience the importance of
teamwork, participation in decision making, responsibility, individual and team development, and commitment to high performance.
The exercise also changes the rhythm of the day and gives all a

chance to get to know the colleagues in their group. This bonding strengthens the feeling of connection with other individuals and identification with the company. The "game" is followed by a video presentation, again stressing how important employees are to Harrah's and outlining the benefits and compensation package. Orders for lunch are then taken, and when the session is over, all adjourn to eat in the employees' cafeteria.

In the afternoon a tour of the facilities includes places not usually seen, such as the bake shop, kitchens, and supply areas. A number of purposes are served by this visit. The new employees get to know where things are and can therefore give directions to customers who ask for them. They learn to find their own way about. They begin to identify with the organization that the facilities symbolize, and they acquire appreciation for the high standards of cleanliness that they see everywhere.

Back in the training room, another videotape is shown about customers: who they are, why they come, and what they consider important during their stay. An employee-relations counselor then outlines employee rights, hearing procedures, rules, promotion policies, and services available through the employee-relations department. Because appearance is critical, Harrah's dress codes are outlined and explained with very clear do's and don'ts.

Finally, the day is summarized, major points are reinforced, and the six-hour orientation session is adjourned.

Phase 2: Assignment to Sponsor: On the first day at work for Harrah's the new employee is assigned to a sponsor. A spokesperson for the company explains the purpose and significance of the system:

> The sponsor's role is to acquaint new employees with their work environment and their fellow employees. We see the sponsor program as a critical link between the motivational orientation program and the often-frightening experience of going to work on the casino floor for the first time. Most of our new hires are from out of the area and are not familiar with the gaming business. We find it important to ease them into it. A sponsor is selected based primarily on attitude and ability to properly develop a rapport with new hires and secondly on knowledge of the company.

The objective is familiarization with the work place, not task training. The sponsor must have a positive attitude toward work and the company, be friendly and able to make the newly hired person feel at home and welcome. Although sponsors receive a financial premium for their services, selection is itself perceived as a reward, and a large number volunteer for the role. Supervisors are never sponsors, but they do choose them. Both bear responsibility for seeing that the new employee is properly introduced, shown around, and given all relevant job-related information. An elaborate checklist must be completed within the first thirty working shifts, dated as done, and initialed by the employee. On completion, this record becomes a part of the employee's permanent personnel file.

Phase 3: Task Training: Finally, new employees receive task training, designed to suit the needs of individual jobs, ranging in length from one to five days for a maid, and four to six weeks for a Twenty-one dealer. Trainers (sometimes the same person as the sponsor) are selected for performance level and knowledge of the job.

Harrah's believes that it has ample, concrete evidence that careful attention to proper integration of new employees pays off. The proof lies in low rates of turnover, high rates of patrons' satisfaction with service, high rate of customers who return, and positive reports from employees themselves. The integration program makes no false promises. It simply prepares the way for high performance by providing the tools to do the job and setting expectations about excellence, pride, ability, self-confidence, identification with the company, and teamwork that are consistently reinforced by the firm's policies and practices. The employee experiences, during recruitment, hiring, orientation, and training the way in which he or she will later be treated on the job.

San Diego Water Utilities Department

The features that best distinguish the orientation and training programs of the San Diego Water Utilities Department are the procedures that produce them. The managerial staff shares responsibility for determining needs and devising methods for meeting them. They budget time for personnel to participate in the programs. Assignment as a "volunteer" instructor to augment the four person Central Safety and Training staff is seen as recognition of superior performance and a reward for it. All employees go through the orientation program together regardless of rank. Division heads and the department's director are on the program. All facilities are toured. Training reinforces what was learned in the orientation program. This is a tale of participation and congruence — congruence between what is told to people in the orientation program, what they experience in it, and what they experience on the job.

Orientation now takes two days. On the first day, instructors cover the department's history, culture, mission, and organizational structure, training and development, safety, education, benefits, and the department's commitment to equal opportunity. The director of utilities is present during a portion of this first day, and each of the six operating divisions, represented by its deputy director, is on the program for forty-five minutes. The participants in the orientation process include new employees at all levels in the department, from the lowest to the highest pay grades. Unskilled employees, professionals, and top-ranking managers mingle to cover the same ground together. Attendance is mandatory, and is followed up to see that all who are scheduled to attend are present. During this first day, everyone is introduced and exercises are conducted to encourage mixing. The importance of teamwork is stressed and reinforced by the effort to help people get to know each other better. The second day of orientation is devoted to a tour of the facilities, including field stations.

Orientation is followed by extensive training in job skills and safe operating practices. The result has been a dramatically improved safety record.

Formal trainers are all utility personnel, and their selection is seen as a reward and recognition for superior performance. Instructors receive no extra pay or direct benefits, but a high percentage of them have received promotions. Further training in the field is conducted under supervision by personnel selected for this task and may continue for three months. Thereafter instruction is not scheduled but is provided as needed.

Three percent of department work hours are devoted annually to training. This amounts to more than 40,000 hours of employee development annually. Some time ago the department arrived at the

3 percent figure by accepting recommendations by thirty supervisors, who were convened as a committee to assess the department's training needs. More recently, twenty department heads met to plan the structure of a new utilities academy, through which new employees will be given two weeks of indoctrination and general training. This program is followed by an additional two weeks of skill training to prepare workers for the jobs to which they will be assigned.

The department's orientation and training programs are effective and a strong testament to the participative process to which they are indebted.

GENERAL ELECTRIC — AIRCRAFT ENGINE BUSINESS GROUP (AEBG)

General Electric, at its Aircraft Engine Business Group plant in Evandale, Ohio, employing 18,000 people, conducts a one-day orientation program for all new employees. The activity, however, is no longer called new-hire orientation because some employees may have been at work for as long as four weeks before they participate in it. It is formal and highly structured, clipping along at a fast pace for 200 to 300 participants in the room at one time. No segment exceeds thirty minutes except the material on compensation and performance appraisal, which takes up to one hour. Presenters are managers themselves, including a senior level executive who emphasizes the company's insistence on high ethical standards of conduct.

After a welcome to the division, and introduction to General Electric through a videotape, information is presented on the organization's structure, company history, and product line. For presentations on compensation and performance appraisal, and for lunch, the audience separates into exempt and nonexempt groups and then reconvenes to cover material on affirmative action, educational opportunities, the tuition refund program, security practices, and benefits. The day ends with a summary and evaluation. On a four-point scale, the average score on satisfaction with the orientation is 3.8.

GENERAL ELECTRIC — NEW MANAGER ASSIMILATION PROGRAM

Since 1978, General Electric has had a New Manager Assimilation Program available on a voluntary basis to managers who are entering a new position anywhere in the company. Bearing some similarity to the supervisory transition that we described in Chapter 10, it is a structured way of shortening the integration time for a new manager, and to avoid many of the problems that arise when the procedure unfolds by chance.

These are the stated objectives in General Electric's approach to new-manager assimilation:

- Enhance communication between new manager and employees
- Establish positive work-group relations
  a) feeling of trust
  b) okay to talk about problems
  c) base for further team growth
- Give team opportunity to learn about new manager without trial-and-error approach
  a) operating style
  b) values
  c) history
- Shorten learning curve on priority issues

The procedure is outlined in Figure 11.1 which follows on the next page.

Step 1: A trained facilitator from the Organization and Staffing (O&S) Department meets with the new manager, explains the procedure, and offers him or her the choice of participating or not. Kate Donnelly, manager of Organization and Staffing at G.E. in Bridgeport, Connecticut, reports that she has never been turned down. How free the choice is for a new manager, however, is an open question. One manager who found the experience very helpful and never considered refusing thought that the option to refuse wasn't really open to him. He believed that failure to participate would make superiors wonder about his courage and disappoint subordinates, especially if it violated their expectation that he would engage in the program. He thought that a new manager who refused to participate would start the job with a handicap.

Step 2: The new manager calls a meeting of his or her staff with the representative from the O&S department who will later facilitate the meeting. He or she announces the meeting and his or her com-

Figure 11.1 New Manager (NM) Assimilation Process

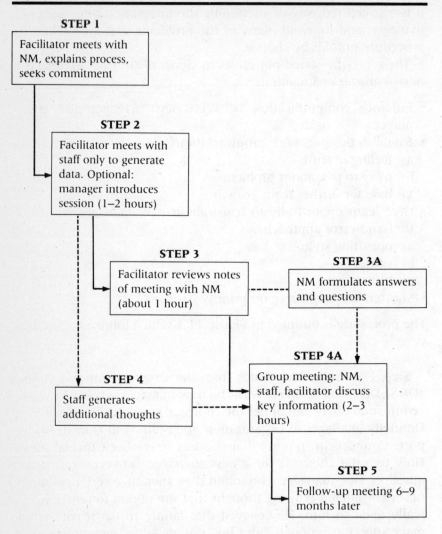

STEP 1
Facilitator meets with
NM, explains process,
seeks commitment

STEP 2
Facilitator meets with
staff only to generate
data. Optional:
manager introduces
session (1–2 hours)

STEP 3
Facilitator reviews notes
of meeting with NM
(about 1 hour)

STEP 3A
NM formulates answers
and questions

STEP 4
Staff generates
additional thoughts

STEP 4A
Group meeting: NM,
staff, facilitator discuss
key information (2–3
hours)

STEP 5
Follow-up meeting 6–9
months later

mitment to it, and makes a brief statement urging everyone to be candid and open. The new manager then leaves. Using the following questions as a guide, the staff, with the help of the facilitator, develops a list of issues it would like to have the new manager discuss. The facilitator records the comments on flip charts that will be shared with the new manager.

QUESTIONS FOR GROUP MEETING:

1. What do we know about (new manager's name)?
2. What would we like to know about (new manager's name)?
3. What are our concerns about _____ becoming our new manager?
4. What _____ needs to know about us as a group.
5. What are the major problems and challenges _____ will be facing during the first year?

Step 2(a): Staff members continue to think about the discussion after the meeting and individually develop other questions that they would like the new manager to answer.

Step 3: During this interval, the facilitator reviews the flip-chart notes taken in the staff session with the new manager and helps him or her think through the answers and questions he or she would like to ask the staff.

Step 3(a): The new manager formulates answers to the questions presented to him or her by the facilitator.

Step 4: The staff meets with the new manager and the facilitator to hear the manager answer the questions formulated in the first staff meeting, to answer his or her questions, to engage in any discussion that ensues, and to develop key issues that will have to be faced in the months to come.

Step 5: Six to nine months later, the same group reconvenes with the facilitator to take a new reading on the group's status. These questions help to focus the discussion:

New-Manager Assimilation — Follow-up

1. What is he or she doing that we like and want him or her to continue or do more of?
2. What is he or she doing which we dislike and which we want him or her to discontinue or to modify?
3. What is he or she not doing that we want him or her to start doing?

Here the formal program ends and the manager, no longer "new," continues to interact with his or her staff in ways that he or she deems appropriate to the group's needs, skills, and resources. All the managers we interviewed who had participated in the program felt very positive about it. They were glad they had used it and believed it had accelerated and contributed to their successful entry into their new positions. The following quotations (respondents' names are disguised) are selected to reflect both the positive feelings about the program that our respondents expressed and some cauonary comments:

Tom: I liked it. Hidden issues get out so that you don't get hit by surprise. It makes you a part of the team faster. Your acceptance or rejection is settled quickly, right at the start. Although I could have and would have taken the time to talk to all my staff individually, the NMA process saves time. You get asked what you wouldn't hear from an individual alone because he or she would be afraid to ask it. In a group, it comes from everyone. I didn't see any negative sides to it. For me, it was only positive.

Jim: I had some apprehension before the meeting, but I think this is only natural. I had some concern that questions would be asked that I couldn't answer. It turned out that some questions were difficult, but I managed well enough with them. However, a first-time manager with less self-confidence might have had more trouble. The meeting gave me an opportunity to talk about what was important to me as a manager, to explain what I expected from them, as well as to learn about the issues that were on their minds. They did tell me about some things that were bothering them, and later I was able to do something about them. Everyone liked the new arrangements much better. The experience was very positive for me. It made communications between us more open, and made relationships easier afterward. I left with a great feeling.

Larry: There are risks. There is a tendency to bring grievances up that have been carried for a long time. I don't think that is particularly appropriate, but then it is an open session. Anything can be brought up. One was mentioned in my meeting, and I listened. It wasn't something I could do anything about, and it just died. I guess the group was doing some testing — and maybe that's to be expected.

Dick: For someone who has a dictatorial style of management, the process might present some problems. He or she would get pretty exposed.

The interesting fact about the cautionary comments is that they are hypothetical. The reservations that were expressed were stated for the benefit of hypothetical people who faced some hypothetical circumstances. In fact, we found no one who had undergone an unpleasant or negative experience.

Lakewood Automotive Assembly Plant — G.M.[2]

All new employees at G.M.'s Lakewood Automotive Assembly Plant, which produces Chevrolet Chevettes and Pontiac T-1000s, go through a basic-training program at Lakewood University, a collection of eight portable classrooms in the unused truck-assembly part of the plant. The training has three main parts:

1. Information about the business and goals for it which a joint union (UAW)-management committee has been established.
2. Interpersonal skills building in areas such as consensus attainment, communication, and conflict resolution.
3. A video series by the Pacific Institute entitled "New Age Thinking."

The training program was designed to prepare employees to start up the Lakewood plant in 1984 after it had been out of production for a year because of declining car sales. The plant reopening was the culmination of a remarkable and successful effort by union and management to restructure their relationship. From a reputation as a plant with many grievances and a troubled inner-city labor history, it has become known as a model for labor-management partnership. The pre-startup training was a critical component in the effort to change. The requirement that all new employees also go through the program increased the likelihood that the new practices would be maintained and further reinforce the behaviors expected of *all* employees, including managers. Joint committees have put together a substantial array of training packages, including:

- a three-day human-interactions workshop intended to improve skills in helping solve and manage conflict.
- a two-day workshop on work-group effectiveness.
- a one-day workshop on how to lead meetings.
- a three-day workshop on goal setting with a report on goal performance by the joint committees, held quarterly for all employees.
- a one-week workshop on departmental functions, procedures, and operational assignments for all employees in their own departments.

Patricia Carrigan, plant manager of the General Motors plant in Bay City, Michigan, was a leading figure in the developments at Lakewood. In a recent article she wrote that, "We had jointly enhanced the skills of more than 3,000 employees, giving them collectively in excess of 360,000 hours of training."[3] Union officials, managers, and workers themselves, trained as facilitators, are responsible for conducting these classes. Thus they are the ones who later must fulfill the expectations they create, a strategy that generates real commitment. At Lakewood, everyday customs and practices reinforce what new employees learn in the two-week, pre-start training program. This is orientation and follow-up at its best.

An Oil Company — Marketing Division

In this oil company, district marketing managers were rotated frequently — almost every three years — as a part of a plan to enhance development of bright, ambitious young people. Although newcomers brought energy and new ideas with them, they also disrupted teamwork and sometimes had difficulty adjusting to differences in the work place and community. Families suffered, as well as employees. Teamwork in the districts was needed because planners, salespeople, controllers, and marketers depended on one another. Some employees managed the transitions more effectively than others and were more productive as a consequence. Taking what was learned from them and adding elements that made sense, one of the authors, as consultant to the oil company, developed a procedure that seemed to hold hope as a standard transition process for all the districts. It had three parts:

1. A meeting to take a norms census.
2. Another meeting to celebrate the departure of people who were leaving.
3. Compilation at that meeting of a list of things that needed to be done to make integration of new employees into the team and their families into the community easier, with assigned responsibilities to effect this transition.

The norms census that we have discussed proceeded smoothly. Some norms, it was discovered, hindered performance, and steps were taken to correct them. The exercise served very useful purposes. It intensified commitment to the team, even for those who were about to leave; increased appreciation for the positive effects on performance of a smooth transition; and provided a checklist that would be shown to new arrivals. Strengthening the attachment of persons who are about to leave appears at first to be at cross-purposes with the need to prepare them and their colleagues for separation. One would think it natural and desirable for persons leaving to gradually separate themselves from the group. Both parties would then begin to get used to doing without each other, making the departure easier. In fact, under the circumstances, "mourning" is often covert or denied, and therefore left unfinished, generating unconscious resentment toward the replacement. Helping well-liked, valued employees to be productive to the very end is healthy on two counts. First, the departing member has the satisfaction of continuing to make a contribution to performance, thus avoiding the feelings of humiliation that often accompany lame-duck status. Second, the people who are left behind are forced to confront the impending loss directly. They can see what they are losing and can openly acknowledge it. By consciously recognizing what they are giving up, they can celebrate the memory, mourn the loss, and prepare for the successor. As a result, workers are likely to have less residual, unconscious resentment toward a replacement. By participating in the plans to welcome the replacement, permission is granted to those who remain to accept the newcomer.

The norms census was followed by a second meeting, devoted to the changing of the guard. The agenda required shifting attention from the departing member to the newcomer. The meeting therefore started with a celebration, marked by expressions of good feeling, shared memories, and displays of affection toward the person who was leaving. Then the group focused on the arriving person's needs. It was the members' responsibility to integrate the newcomer and his or her family into the work place and community.

To accomplish its purpose, the group chose to answer the question, "What would *I* like to have done for *me* when going to a new job in a new place? By looking at themselves, they enhanced their connection with newcomers. The newcomers became individuals with whom each person in the group could identify. The task also drew on one's own experience with entry, both good and bad, and increased commitment to developing procedures that might later be useful when moving to another district.

This list was produced from responses to the assignments that people were given:

What I Would Like to Know When I Go
to a New Job — New Place
(Persons responsible for informing a newcomer in parentheses)

1. My boss' expectations of me. (*boss*)
2. What are my responsibilities? (*boss*)
3. What resources are available to me to accomplish my task — people, facilities, equipment, and office? (*boss, peers, staff*)
4. What current projects are important: front-burner items, establishing priorities? (*boss, peers, staff*)
5. Establish relationships — peers, subordinates. Two-way street. (*all members of the team, self*)
6. How does my role fit into the organization's scheme of things? (*boss, peers*)
7. Information about district — the business — what is it? (*boss, peers*)
8. Talk about area: information and help in getting around, meeting critical people in the community, schools, shopping, housing, transportation. Bring spouse aboard — welcome. (*boss, peers, spouse of boss, peers*)
   Help spouse to find job if employment is sought. (*boss, peers, staff*)

9. Introduction to management-team concept — introduction to the norms (*boss, all members of the team*)
10. Invite to lunch first few days. (*all members of the team*)

Results of the transition process were positive. Departing members left feeling better than they ever had, feeling appreciated to the end and maintaining productivity. Newcomers expressed considerable satisfaction with the way they were welcomed. They found that they integrated faster at work, felt more productive, and were pleased with the more rapid adjustment of their families to the new environment. Family members expressed surprise and pleasure at the way in which they were greeted, and reported that their warm welcome led to friendships that they believed they would retain. Oldtimers liked the program and said that because of it they had an easier time saying goodbye to those who were leaving and accepting the ones who took their place. It was their belief that the change-overs were smoother than ever before. Performance did not seem to suffer during the time newcomers were learning the ropes; many more ideas were offered by them than had been usual, and they received favorable treatment rather than being kept at some distance until they had proven themselves, as in the past.

The process was unique in a number of respects. First, it took advantage of the managers' own experiences to identify the information and help that newcomers needed. Second, specific individuals were assigned the responsibility to see that newcomers got that information and help. Third, the need to help newcomers and their families integrate into the community was recognized, with very positive effects on performance at work.

As important as it is to pay attention to the newcomers' entry into the community, it is generally neglected, a point underscored by a manager from NASA who wrote to us as follows:

It can sometimes be difficult for new people moving here, many times without benefit of friends or family. This organization could be instrumental in helping with that adjustment, which could include:

- Regular get-togethers to network with other participants who have similar interests, to establish more of a sense of community and a sense of common purpose.
- Information on what the area has to offer.

- Information on locating and using local informational resources.

THE BUDDY SYSTEM

We have mentioned the buddy system as a practical way of seeing
that a newcomer learns all he or she needs to know from a seasoned
veteran with a good attitude who knows what is going on. Bruce
Posner describes the experiences of a number of small companies
that rely on variations on the buddy system to break in new
employees.[4]

> The Charrette Corporation in Woburn, Massachusetts, a commercial
> art and office-products supply company with 200 employees, assigns
> new hires to the care of a "good experienced coworker for a month
> or two."
>
> W. L. Gore & Associates, Inc., the maker of patented "Gore-tex,"
> a versatile fabric often used in cold-weather gear for insulation and
> weather protection, has "new 'associates' (as employees are called)
> take a long voyage through the business before settling into their own
> position, regardless of the specific job for which they were hired."[5]
>
> Skyway Freight Systems, an express delivery company in San
> Francisco with seventy employees, calls its buddy system "walking
> in the other person's moccasins." "During the first week, each new-
> comer follows a customer order from pickup through delivery and
> learns about every aspect of data entry, tracking, and billing. New
> employees meet coworkers throughout the company, and see how
> the various functional areas interact with one another."[6]

The buddy system is an old idea, perhaps the oldest of orientation
approaches, having its foundation in apprenticeship. When orientation was no longer associated with the training needed to acquire
a given standard of skill in a craft, its use in industry began to disappear. Certainly it is time-consuming, and therefore expensive.
How much time and resources should be devoted to personal guidance under a buddy's tutelage depends on the importance and complexity of the job. But given the cost of turnover, in loss of skilled
help, expense of hiring, and disruption to the organization, it appears that a lot more use of buddies can be justified.

THE NEED

We are a society on the move. Every year, on the average, twenty million Americans change jobs[7], and another six million enter the labor force. Thus, on each work day approximately one hundred thousand persons, or one out of five people in this country experience their first day at work.[8]

In the last few years, the country's larger companies each relocated almost 200 executives a year, at an average direct, measurable cost in current dollars of about $34,000, excluding the intangible costs associated with breaking in on the new job. Included in that figure were transportation costs, losses on home sales, allowances to cover higher purchase cost of a comparable home in the new location, cost-of-living allowances, interest-rate assistance, and assistance with mortgage down payments. Contrary to expectations in the late 1970s and early 1980s, when it was widely predicted that the new breed of "yuppie" professionals would resist moving in order to preserve their life-styles, aspiring Americans have stayed in motion. The phenomenon shows no signs of diminishing as competition for better jobs among the large cohort of baby boomers in their thirties intensifies, and corporations continue to build relocation into their plans for career development and effective use of personnel.

Such mobility presents an opportunity and a problem. The opportunity lies in the hope that springs in the heart of most newcomers. For them the first day on the job is their chance for a fresh start. The organization can take advantage of this favorable attitude, but it can be lost if left to chance encounters. Observing the extent to which organizations waste this opportunity, some cynics have said that the first day at work is the last time that the average employer sees the ideal employee (and vice versa).

VALUE OF ORIENTATION PROGRAMS

As you can see in the orientation programs described in this chapter, a variety of effective approaches to the problem are available. It is our impression, however, that results are directly related to the care that goes into the design and maintenance of the program. New employees are the building blocks, through whom organizations lay the foundation for their future. If care is taken to build properly, the structure that rises will be strong, reliable, and enduring. That is the lesson we have learned from our study. The lesson is clear, and yet it seems to be lost on many organizations, who ignore it at their peril. Given the high volume of job turnover that most companies experience, however, opportunities abound for significant new beginnings. It is never too late to design a good orientation program. We hope that this chapter will help those whose organizations don't have orientation programs to design them, and those who do have them to make theirs even better.

AFTERWORD

W E will have fulfilled our objectives if, after reading this book, you, as a newcomer, will know how to cope better with the pitfalls of newness, coworkers will be able to help the new member adapt to their group faster, supervisors will understand new workers' needs and ease their transition, and organizations will create a process that will facilitate the effective integration of newcomers.

We believe that everyone, no matter in what position, can make a real difference in their own adjustment and comfort when starting a new job, as well as in the adjustment and comfort of others. Every one of us is part of a long chain of people who can improve the ways in which "the new kid on the block" is helped to fit in.

LOSE/WIN

I have known the pain of
failure
frustration
disappointment
defeat

Because I have taken a chance on
winning
succeeding
achieving

It takes a lot of the first
to get some of the second.

APPENDIX A

The following is a survey we used to test male and female responses to hazing. Note that the name "Chris" was used in one third of the questionnaires, "Christine" in another third, and "Christopher" in the last third.

After three months of struggling through countless tests and interviews, Chris was finally hired as a ticket agent by Reliable Airlines. The job offered only average pay and little mental challenge, yet it was highly sought after because of the attractive fringe benefits, like free flights and generous discounts on hotels and tours. Chris had to compete with many applicants for the few available positions.

After two weeks of training at the corporate headquarters, Chris was assigned to a job. During the first month on the job, these incidents occurred:

Chris arrived at work one morning and noticed two other agents punching their own timecards as well as those of two friends who were obviously late for work. As they punched the cards of their tardy coworkers, one of them looked at Chris and asked in a defiant tone, "Hey Chris, are you going to go tell the boss on us?" The agents looked at each other and laughed as they walked to their work stations.

During the first month on the job, Chris noticed that many of the most menial tasks were delegated to the station that Chris worked from. Chris also worked the least desirable evening and weekend shifts more frequently than anyone else. Chris also noticed that the other agents freely swapped days off with each other so that they could take advantage of the free flights and other travel discounts. Yet when Chris tried to swap a day off, the other agents responded with a cool and noncommittal answer.

One day during the first month of work, Chris locked up the ticket drawer as company security regulations required before leaving the counter to go on a break. Instead of taking the key, Chris forgot and left it on a shelf below the ticket drawer. The other agents saw Chris put the key on the shelf and one of them picked it up and hid it. When Chris returned from the break and began to search for the key, the agents giggled and snickered as Chris's search became increasingly frantic. Finally, as the line of impatient customers grew long, one of the agents tossed the key to Chris and innocently asked, "Oh, were you looking for this?" During the lunch breaks for the next few days, the other agents made jokes about Chris losing the key, and several imitated Chris's frantic search for the key, to the amusement of the others in the lunchroom.

1. What do you think has occurred in the case that you have just read about?

2. What do you think might be the purpose behind these incidents?

3. If these incidents happened to you, how would you react?

4. What do you believe would be the consequences of your having reacted in this way?

5. Would you take part in creating an incident like this one?

6. Do you see a positive or negative outcome resulting from these incidents? Please explain.

7. Please answer the following:

   Age: _____ Sex: _____ Level in college: _____

   Work experience (please check one):

   0 to 1 year   ☐
   1 to 5 years   ☐
   5 or more years   ☐

   Type of work performed:

8. During your work experience, have you ever participated in hazing, as either a giver or a receiver? Please describe the events in detail.

a. What was done *to you* or *by you* or both?

b. How did you react?

c. What was the result of your reaction?

APPENDIX B

The following is a sample questionnaire we used to test the effectiveness of new employees' orientation.

QUESTIONNAIRE ON FIRST DAYS AT WORK

Male ☐   Female ☐   Age _____
Caucasian ☐   Black ☐   Hispanic ☐   Asian ☐   Other ☐
Hourly Worker: Blue Collar ☐   Hourly: White Collar ☐
Professional ☐   Managerial ☐   Other ☐

Type of Job _____

Type of Organization _____

How Long in Present Job _____

Position _____

Your Employment Status: Full Time ☐   Part Time ☐
Temporary Worker ☐   on Flexible Working Hours ☐

When you were hired by the company you're working for now, what did your immediate supervisor do that made it easier for you to fit in?

What did he or she do that made it harder?

What did your coworkers do to make it easier for you to fit in?

What did they do that made it harder?

What did you do yourself that made it easier?

What did you do that made it harder?

How quickly were you made to feel welcome in your work group?
Immediately ☐   A few days ☐   Weeks ☐   Months ☐
Never ☐

What could have been done and by whom to make you feel welcome in your work group more quickly?

How do you feel today about your coworkers?

How do you feel about your immediate supervisor?

How do you feel about the company you're working for?

Do you think your first few days and weeks influenced your sub-sequent attitude at work? Yes ☐   No ☐   If yes, in what way and for how long?

If your company has an orientation program, can you describe it (or include a copy of it with this questionnaire)? Did it help you get integrated better or faster?

What is your most lasting memory of your first days at work?

If you would like your company to be given credit in our book, please give us the name and address.

If you are willing to be interviewed about your early experiences as a new employee, please give us your name, address, phone number, and best time to reach you.

Do you have any further thoughts, comments, suggestions that may be helpful to us?

NOTES

Chapter 1

[1]John A. Tenkins, "A Candid Talk with Justice Blackmun," *New York Times Magazine,* Feb. 20, 1983, pp. 20–26.

[2]Leonard Zunin, M.D., with Natalie Zunin, *Contact: The First Four Minutes* (New York: Ballantine Books, 1972).

Charlene Mitchell and Thomas Burdick, "First Impressions Last," *Savvy* (August 1985), pp. 32–35.

[3]"The Money Chase," *Time* (May 4, 1984).

Chapter 2

[1]*The American Heritage Dictionary* (Boston: Houghton Mifflin, 1975).

[2]Katherine Stechert, "Can't You Take a Joke?" *Savvy* (June 1986).

[3]Rose Laub Coser, "Laughter Among Colleagues" (Boston: McLean Hospital, Belmont, Mass.)

[4]*The Wall Street Journal,* Dec. 8, 1983.

[5]Marc Appleman, "Chargers' Hazing Days of Summer Are Nearly Gone," *Los Angeles Times,* Aug. 2, 1984.

[6]*The Wall Street Journal,* Jan. 22, 1982.

[7]Richard Pascale, "Fitting New Employees into the Company Culture," *Fortune* (May 28, 1984), p. 30.

[8]Victor Turner, "Variation on a Theme of Liminality," Amsterdam's Secular Ritual Association.

[9]James L. Brain, "Sex, Incest and Death: Initiation Rites Reconsidered," *Current Anthropology,* 18, no. 2 (June 1977).

[10]Victor Turner, "Variations on a Theme."

[11]Arnold Van Gennep, *The Rites of Passage* (Chicago: University of Chicago Press, 1960).

[12]*Ibid.* Van Gennep.

Chapter 3

[1]*Cases on Women in Management* (Simmons College, Graduate College of Management), 1976, pp. 79–80.

[2]*Lower Income Women Tell of Their Lives and Struggles,* "Dignity," Oral Histories Compiled by Fran Leepr Buss (Ann Arbor: University of Michigan Press, 1985).

[3]G. Fine, "Sociological Approaches to the Study of Humor," in Paul McGhee

and Jeffrey Goldstern, eds., *Handbook of Humor Research,* (vol. I) Basic Issues (New York: Springer-Verlag, 1983).

⁴Carol A. Mitchell, "The Difference Between Male and Female Joke-Telling as Exemplified in a College Community," *Dissertation Abstracts International,* vol. 37 (February 1977), pp. 1–10, 5270.

⁵*Sexual Harassment in the Federal Government.* Hearings by the Post Office and Civil Service Committee, Oct. 23, Nov. 13, 1979. Serial 96-57 (Washington, D.C.: U.S. Government Printing Office, 1980).

⁶Robert F. Priest, "The Future of Sexist Humor in the Work Place." Paper given at the 1984 Western Humor and Irony Membership Conference on Contemporary Humor, Phoenix, Ariz., March 31, 1984.

⁷*The Wall Street Journal,* Feb. 3, 1983.

⁸Glenn Loury, "A New American Dilemma: Racial Politics, Black and White," *New Republic* (December 1984), pp. 14–24.

⁹Terry L. Leap and Larry R. Smeltzer, "Racial Remarks in the Workplace: Humor or Harassment?" *Harvard Business Review* (Nov.–Dec. 1984), pp. 74–78.

¹⁰Martin Lasden, "Laughter Gives You an Edge," *Computer Decisions,* vol. 17, no. 8 (April 23, 1985), pp. 70–80.

Chapter 4

¹Natasha Josefowitz, *Is This Where I Was Going?* (New York: Warner Books, 1983).

²Natasha Josefowitz, Instructor's Manual for *Paths to Power,* copyright © 1980. Obtainable from General Publishing Group, Addison-Wesley Publishing Company, Reading, Mass. 01867.

³Richard Pascale, "Fitting New Employees into the Company Culture," *Fortune* (May 28, 1984), pp. 28–30.

Chapter 5

¹For an elaboration of their definition, see: Edgar H. Schein, *Organizational Culture and Leadership* (San Francisco: Jossey-Bass, 1985), p. 9.

²Natasha Josefowitz, *Paths to Power* (Reading, Mass.: Addison-Wesley, 1980), pp. 56–59.

³Daniel L. Isenberg, "How Senior Managers Think," *Harvard Business Review* (Nov.–Dec. 1984).

⁴Natasha Josefowitz, "In Your Heart You Know You're Right: Intuition as a Job Skill," *Ms.* (November 1984).

Chapter 6

¹John P. Kotter, Victor A. Faux, and Charles McArthur, *Self-Assessment and Career Development* (Englewood Cliffs, N.J.: Prentice-Hall, 1978).

²Meryl Reis Louis, "Career Transitions: Varieties and Commonalities," *Academy of Management Review,* vol. 5, no. 3 (1980), pp. 329–340.

³Bernard Weiner, *Achievement, Motivation, and Attribution Theory* (Morristown, N.J.: General Learning Press, 1974).

[4]Meryl Reis Louis, "Surprise and Sense Making: What Newcomers Experience in Entering Unfamiliar Organizational Settings," *Administrative Science Quarterly* (June 1980), pp. 225–251.

[5]John P. Kotter, Victor A. Faux, and Charles McArthur, *Self-Assessment and Career Development* (Englewood Cliffs, N.J.: Prentice-Hall, 1978), pp. 168–169.

[6]Fernando Bartolome and Paul A. Lee Evans, "Must Success Cost So Much?" *Harvard Business Review* (March–April 1980), pp. 142–143.

[7]Meryl Reis Louis, "Managing Career Transitions: A Missing Link in Career Development," *Organizational Dynamics* (Spring 1982), pp. 68–77.

[8]Meryl Louis, "Career Transitions," pp. 225–251.

[9]D. Eden and A. B. Shani, "Pygmalion Goes to Boot Camp: Expectancy, Leadership and Trainee Performance," *Journal of Applied Psychology,* 67 (1982), pp. 194–199.

Chapter 7

[1]Natasha Josefowitz, *Is This Where I Was Going?* (New York: Warner Books, 1983).

[2]Natasha Josefowitz, unpublished poem.

[3]Barbara Benedict Bunker, *The Toll of Travel: Separation and Reunion.* State University of New York at Buffalo. Unpublished manuscript, 1982.

[4]Lynne F. McGee and Elie Blake, "Moving On," *Savvy* (November 1985), pp. 37–44.

Chapter 8

[1]"The Case of Eddy Martin" has been disguised to protect the anonymity of the people involved.

[2]Solomon Asch, "Opinions and Social Pressure," *Scientific American,* 193(5) (1955), pp. 31–35.

Chapter 9

[1]Alvin W. Gouldner, "The Norm of Reciprocity: A Preliminary Statement," *American Sociological Review,* 25 (1966), pp. 161–169.

[2]Donald F. Roy, "Banana Time, Job Satisfaction and Informal Interaction," *Human Organization,* 18(4) (1959), pp. 158–169.

[3]Elisabeth Kübler-Ross, *On Death and Dying* (New York: Macmillan Publishing Co., 1969).

Chapter 10

[1]Robert I. Sutton and Meryl R. Louis, "The Influence of Selection and Socialization on Insider Sense-Making." Stanford University School of Management, Technical Report #84-6, September 1984.

[2]Adapted from the City of San Diego "Supervisor's New Employee Information Checklist," 1985.

[3]Natasha Josefowitz, *You're the Boss! Managing with Understanding and Effectiveness* (New York: Warner Books, 1985).

[4]Sutton and Louis, "Influence of Selection and Socialization."

[5]Michael D. Mitchell, "The Transition Meeting: A Technique When Changing Managers," *Harvard Business Review* (May–June 1976).

Also refer to: Raymond J. Zugel, "Managing Supervisory Transition," *The 1983 Annual for Facilitators, Trainers and Consultants,* ed. by Goodstein and Pfeiffer (San Diego: University Associates, 1983).

Chapter 11

[1]Natasha Josefowitz, unpublished poem.

[2]Patricia M. Carrigan, "Up from the Ashes," *O.D. Practitioner,* vol. 18, no. 1 (March 1986).

[3]Carrigan, "Up from the Ashes."

[4]Bruce G. Posner, "The First Day on the Job," *INC.* (June 1985), pp. 73–75.

[5]Posner, "First Day."

[6]Posner, "First Day."

[7]Posner, "First Day."

[8]Statistical Abstracts of the United States Bureau of Census, 1987.

[9]Statistical Yearbook of Immigration and Naturalization Service, Department of Justice, 1986.

INDEX